Worship and Waste

Worship and Waste

A Christological Companion to the Book of 2 Samuel

DANIEL J. D. STULAC

CASCADE *Books* • Eugene, Oregon

WORSHIP AND WASTE
A Christological Companion to the Book of 2 Samuel

Copyright © 2025 Daniel J. D. Stulac. All rights reserved. Except for brief quotations in critical publications or reviews, no part of this book may be reproduced in any manner without prior written permission from the publisher. Write: Permissions, Wipf and Stock Publishers, 199 W. 8th Ave., Suite 3, Eugene, OR 97401.

Cascade Books
An Imprint of Wipf and Stock Publishers
199 W. 8th Ave., Suite 3
Eugene, OR 97401

www.wipfandstock.com

PAPERBACK ISBN: 979-8-3852-1901-8
HARDCOVER ISBN: 979-8-3852-1902-5
EBOOK ISBN: 979-8-3852-1903-2

Cataloguing-in-Publication data:

Names: Stulac, Daniel J. (Daniel John) [author].

Title: Worship and waste : a christological companion to the book of 2 Samuel / by Daniel J. D. Stulac.

Description: Eugene, OR: Cascade Books, 2025 | Includes bibliographical references.

Identifiers: ISBN 979-8-3852-1901-8 (paperback) | ISBN 979-8-3852-1902-5 (hardcover) | ISBN 979-8-3852-1903-2 (ebook)

Subjects: LCSH: Bible.—Samuel, 2nd—Criticism, interpretation, etc. | David, King of Israel. | Bible—Hermeneutics.

Classification: s1325.53 s78 2025 (paperback) | s1325.53 (ebook)

VERSION NUMBER 07/15/25

All Old Testament Scripture quotations and paraphrases are the author's original work.

All New Testament Scripture quotations are taken from the Holy Bible, New International Version®, NIV®. Copyright © 1973, 1978, 1984, 2011 by Biblica, Inc.™ Used by permission of Zondervan. All rights reserved worldwide. www.zondervan.com The "NIV" and "New International Version" are trademarks registered in the United States Patent and Trademark Office by Biblica, Inc.™

for Danielle
love heals wounds

Contents

	Author's Note: How to Read This Book	ix
1	Mark You the Floor? (2 Samuel 1)	1
2	An Eye for an Eye (2 Samuel 2–4)	10
3	A Is for Achievement, D Is for Dance (2 Samuel 5–8)	28
4	Promises, Promises (2 Samuel 10–12)	40
5	Epiphany Cake (2 Samuel 9)	57
6	Betrayed by a Kiss (2 Samuel 13–16)	69
7	Hanging from a Tree (2 Samuel 17–20)	88
8	Worship and Waste (2 Samuel 21–24)	101
	Postlude	114
	Endnotes	117
	Bibliography	121

Author's Note

How to Read This Book

THIS BOOK IS THE final installment in a three-volume series. While *Gift of the Grotesque: A Christological Companion to the Book of Judges* and *Tragedy of the Commons: A Christological Companion to the Book of 1 Samuel* do not constitute prerequisite reading for every person who may be interested in *Worship and Waste*, they do provide important context for the exegetical essays contained within. For in the same way that 2 Samuel closely relates to 1 Samuel (with respect to compositional history, literary form, and theological content), *Worship and Waste* likewise picks up precisely where *Tragedy* left off—with the unmitigated disaster of Saul's reign, ending in suicide. Especially attentive readers may notice that while *Tragedy* begins with two preludes, it does not contain a postlude (by contrast, both a prelude and a postlude appear in *Gift*). In my effort to honor the two Samuels' canonical continuity, *Worship and Waste* dives into David's story without introduction, and with Saul's ignominious death hopefully still vivid in the reader's mind. No prelude to get you started, in other words—read *Tragedy of the Commons* instead. That said, a postlude, intended to serve as a conclusion for both *Tragedy* and *Worship*, appears at the end of the present volume.

Like the first two books in the series, *Worship and Waste* is best understood not as a typical Bible commentary—a literary form with which readers may be more familiar—but as a *companion*. By this I mean the following: *Worship and Waste* is "exegetical art" intended to stand alongside Scripture, much like a painting or other visual composition. For this reason, I do not offer the reader an explanation for every verse appearing in 2 Samuel. Nor do I always discuss 2 Samuel's plot in the expected order (for example, see chapters 3, 4, and 5 in the Table of Contents).

Author's Note

Instead, *Worship and Waste* aims to deliver an aesthetic experience that may help to overcome some of the hermeneutical prejudices that many readers bring to Old Testament narrative and that, in my judgment, often discourage life-giving experiences with the text (e.g., that it is moralistic, irrelevant, outdated, etc.). Like a commentary, *Worship and Waste* relies on deeply attentive, rigorous study of the Bible's literary craftsmanship in its original language. Nevertheless, insofar as it constitutes an act of Christian confession, my work concentrates less on the adjudication of scholarly debates and more on how I believe the text prepares its reader to receive the gospel of Jesus Christ. To this point, I reiterate here what I wrote in the Author's Note that introduces *Gift of the Grotesque* and then repeated in the Author's Note that introduces *Tragedy of the Commons*: "We must never lose sight of the fact that the Bible's prophetic, soul-stabbing rhetoric and the standard academese through which that rhetoric is so frequently filtered mix like oil and water. The last thing the Bible wants from its readership is more nitpicking. It desires our unconditional surrender, not our measured reconstruction of the facts." For this reason, *Worship and Waste* expands upon the work I began in *Gift* and continued in *Tragedy*, weaving together a theological interpretation of Scripture with elements of memoir and homily, as well as brief reflections on poetry, film, and contemporary culture. In sum, I have tried to produce writing that is at once personal, relevant, and beautiful—a type of literature like the Bible itself that invites you, the reader, into a fresh encounter with the Old Testament's incarnate, crucified, and resurrected King.

I

Mark You the Floor?

(2 Samuel 1)

Mark you the floor? that square and speckled stone,
Which looks so firm and strong,
Is Patience:
And th' other black and grave, wherewith each one
Is checkered all along,
Humility:
The gentle rising, which on either hand
Leads to the Choir above,
Is Confidence:
But the sweet cement, which in one sure band
Ties the whole frame, is Love
And Charity.
Hither sometimes Sin steals, and stains
The marble's neat and curious veins:
But all is cleansed when the marble weeps.
Sometimes Death, puffing at the door,
Blows all the dust about the floor:
But while he thinks to spoil the room, he sweeps.
Blessed be the Architect, whose art
Could build so strong in a weak heart.

GEORGE HERBERT, "THE CHURCH-FLOOR"

☩

"Here is the man," God said to Samuel when the prophet first laid eyes on Saul (1 Sam 9:17). *Hinneh ha'ish. Idou ho anthrōpos.* And thoroughly human Saul soon proved himself to be: a less-than-divine ruler whom Israel, in its relentless pursuit of false gods, had long desired to enthrone. Here is the man who once towered above his peers but whose impressive stature the Philistines finally cut down to size, making him like Dagon and Goliath—a headless horseman to haunt the remainder of the scroll.

"*Idou ho anthrōpos,*" the Roman governor unwittingly repeated, leaning out over the frothy-mouthed crowd (John 19:5). *Hinneh ha'ish.* Here is the Man who preached Deuteronomy's hope, who carried the infirmities of a people without the eyes to see or the ears to hear or the hearts to break. Here hangs Israel's true king, cut down in his prime by the universal urge to crucify what we do not understand. We torture all that would transform us; we annihilate what most we need; we self-destruct in the moment of our rescue. Here, too, sits the human reader, gazing down into the Old Testament's prophetic mirror. Will your eyes see? Will your ears hear? Will your heart break on these jagged shores, on these ragged words? You are Scripture's target. *Attah ha'ish.* You, too, are the *anthrōpos* it has in mind. "*You* are the man" (2 Sam 12:7).

☩

Huffing and puffing at the door, a disheveled Amalekite arrives at the court of Saul's replacement, the man after God's own heart (1 Sam 13:14; 16:7; see Acts 13:22). Perhaps, at first blush, David saw a bit of himself in the refugee's torn jacket and worn-out shoes, his red face and dirty hair (2 Sam 1:2). "Go on," says the Judean fox, leaning forward from his chair—"tell me everything" (2 Sam 1:4). As the Amalekite relates his story, however, the two characters' stark differences, not their similarities, begin to emerge. Having found a badly wounded Saul on Mount Gilboa, and with the Philistines closing in, the Amalekite did as he was instructed and finished the job (2 Sam 1:6–10). In other words, he performed a mercy killing at Saul's request, and thus came to possesses

> Certainly David, the *anthrōpos* whose personality dominates every page of the book to come, wouldn't murder, would he?

the royal insignia, which he now delivers on bended knee. Listening closely, David shifts his weight and settles back into his seat. Surely the reader remembers that when given the opportunity to eliminate Saul, David twice refrained. The son of Jesse would never dream of doing what this dusty herald of "good news" has apparently done. Never would he take what does not belong to him. Never would he "stretch out his hand against the LORD's Anointed" (2 Sam 1:14). Certainly David, the *anthrōpos* whose personality dominates every page of the book to come, wouldn't *murder*, would he?

The ax falls swiftly. "Your blood is upon your own head," says David, "for you admitted it yourself: 'I put the LORD's Anointed to death'" (2 Sam 1:16). So the Amalekite dies for his crime according to the principle of *lex talionis*—an eye for an eye and a tooth for a tooth. He becomes 2 Samuel's first casualty, its first wasted life. Many more will follow suit before all thirteen tricks are played, but before wading into that carnage, the reader pauses to consider the curiosity of the Amalekite's ill-advised lead. Unlike David, you were there with Saul in 1 Samuel 31, watching in silence as the bodies piled up. You saw the Philistines press their attack; you saw them strike down Saul's three sons (1 Sam 31:1–2). You looked on with rapt attention when the arrows pierced his side, when he ordered his armor bearer to run him through (1 Sam 31:3–4). You held your breath, horrified, as Israel's king, finding no "man of valor" (see 1 Sam 14:52) bold enough to "stretch out his hand against the LORD's Anointed," fell upon his sword (1 Sam 31:4). Nowhere in this scene does the Amalekite of 2 Samuel 1 appear, a narrative gap that feeds directly into the irony of Saul's tragic demise. Paranoid hunter that he was, Saul winds up dead by no one's hand but his own. In sum, the Amalekite has apparently lied to David, and so, like Saul, becomes the collateral damage of his own sin.

Aware of all this, the reader of 2 Samuel 1 finds him- or herself suddenly caught in a riptide of suspicion and doubt. On one hand, 1 Sam 31:4–5 states only that Saul "fell on his sword" and that his armor bearer, at some point later, "saw that Saul was dead." Perhaps the reticent nature of biblical narrative does not exclude the possibility that the Amalekite's version of events could be true as well. On the other hand, it's tough to shake the feeling that, in this book's opening vignette, David's acuity for sussing out his courtiers' deceptions as well as his instinct for fair application of the Law already leaves something to be desired. Should a man really die for confessing to a crime he did not commit? Or if he did act out of obedience as he claims, having spared the king torture and abuse at

Philistine hands, is such a deed truly worthy of capital punishment? Then again, perhaps David knows more (or suspects more) than his superficial credulity lets on. Does it not seem more than a little convenient that Jesse's son—when his notion of justice has been meted out and the dust has settled—winds up with Saul's crown perched upon his head, while the only material witness to this transfer of power lies six feet under and so remains forever beyond the reach of cross-examination? Has the Law, in David's hands, become a pretext through which to pursue his ambitions? Am I confident that I have understood what has just transpired? Strange sand indeed on which to lay a cathedral floor.

☨

Thus the door to a thousand different interpretations of 2 Samuel stands ajar. In blows a stiff, modern gale, aimed squarely at the psychological recesses and hidden motives of the characters in question. Much of the time, the story's refusal to provide explicit information on this front becomes for readers an invitation to pursue endless moral speculation through the interweaving of textual details and inferential assumptions. Gradually the plot coheres from an assemblage of raw materials—archaeology, anthropology, sociology, and narratology—until a protagonist worthy of an eighteenth-century novel is slowly born. David son of Jesse: the best, the worst, or at least the most human king that ancient Israel ever knew. *Realism* comes to act as the mortar that binds the Bible's stained-glass iconography into a book worth reading.

With all due respect to Aharoni and Albright, I will take my cues from the ambiguous Amalekite instead. How should the reader account for the text's undetermined background? What rhetorical and theological purpose do its narrative chasms ultimately serve? As it turns out, a watertight assessment of David's appeal to *lex talionis* in 2 Samuel 1 proves elusive no matter how hard one squints. You may take the Amalekite at his word, but should you? Can you be sure? You may think you know something about him that David does not, but in fabricating his mind (which does not actually exist), you'll soon discover that you know less than you thought, and that perhaps the narrator and David have cuckolded you in the end. Savvy to such propaganda, you may fancy yourself a critic, capable of rising above the story's political disinformation, only to find yourself fumbling about with a painfully selective, childishly naïve reconstruction of the so-called facts. Having reached my forties, and with a degree in hand, I am fairly certain now that the Bible's authors were smarter than I am.

I do not know—and I will never know—if the Amalekite deserves it. I know his life becomes a waste; that much is plain. Here is a man who did not have to die prematurely, someone who easily could have avoided such an outcome had he made different choices along the way. But I do not know how to judge him. Still less do I know how to judge David. I know how to imagine David, for the story's fraught background carves out all the space my brain needs to run amok. But I cannot know him as only God knows him, and as only he knows God. In this admission lies the point of the story's tightlipped refusal to issue moral imperatives through the portrayal of psychologically complete characters. Its gaps exist not to be filled with finger-wagging speculation, but with compassion. Not with "brave" realism or proto-humanism, but with patience, humility, and love. Narrative gaps are a form of pedagogy, of spiritual and theological formation, intended to shape their students into persons less like me and more like the One who illumines the velum scroll from behind. They dress down the narcissist in me; they drape upon me invisible clothes. They expose the secret sociopath who is ever hatching plans, working the room, and calculating results. Not modern realism, but interpretive *charity* cements this house's marble frame, undergirded by the rueful recognition that I am no better than the liars and murderers on the page. Is it too early in this little hermeneutical experiment of mine to claim—and will I lose my scholarly reputation for it?—that the interpretive space Old Testament narrative opens up should be filled neither by the self-assured preacher nor by the educated critic, but by the Son of Man?

To read a Former Prophet (i.e., Joshua–2 Kings, excluding Ruth) is to come face to face with the scathing indictment of Isa 1:5: "Your whole head is sick! Your whole heart, diseased!" The book of Joshua describes a theologically unified people in possession of the Promised Land, but against this ideal backdrop, Israel's fortunes steadily fall apart. Why should anyone want to suffer through such cheerless literature, where each book proves more woebegone than the last? Why read the stories of cheats and liars, of idolators and tax collectors, whose intransigence sends them, predictably, into exile? The answer to this question, I believe, has to do with the fact that each of these books takes its direction from Deuteronomy 30. Each has been dipped in the vision of Jeremiah 31. Each performs like the scalpel Jesus eventually deploys in Matthew 5. In other words, each Former

Prophet has been designed to break its reader's heart, to scrape out the fat, and to sew it up again. The great tragedies of the Old Testament lead their readers into deep contemplation of Isaiah's most profound, theological claim: "Zion through justice shall be redeemed . . ." (Isa 1:27). Israel's redemption comes about not because God sweeps sin under the rug. Neither does God shrug his shoulders while observing, with a forlorn sigh, that "boys will be boys." Rather, redemption occurs when God inhabits human failure, flipping it upside down and pulling it inside out. Zion's salvation unfolds through the consequences of Zion's sin. Who could have guessed? Hope conceals itself in the last place anyone would think to look; it hides deep inside the belly of Jonah's whale. Resurrection wells up from within Scripture's exilic tragedy, not from without.

> To read a Former Prophet is to come face to face with the scathing indictment of Isa 1:5: "Your whole head is sick! Your whole heart, diseased!"

The prophetic book of 2 Samuel expresses this transformational truth through narrative in the same way that Isaiah expresses it through lyric verse. The protagonist and murderer whose personality dominates this text survives his own story only because God performs a gracious mystery on his behalf—in, through, and ultimately beyond the principle of *lex talionis*. Thus the story's psychological gaps invite neither moral calculation nor self-righteous indignation, despite the fact that many readers stuff them with precisely that. They invite tears. If you can weep for Saul (2 Sam 1:24), 2 Samuel's implied author intimates, then perhaps you can weep for David, too. For indeed, none of his accomplishments will stand the test of time. Everything will be lost. Everything will be stripped away. The kingship, the castle, and the court; the music, the melodies, and the admirers; the wealth, the women, and the wine. What remains of a House when it goes into exile, when Saul's royal diadem mutates overnight into a crown of thorns? "Truly I tell you, not one stone here will be left on another; every one will be thrown down" (Matt 24:2). Good God—what a book! What a story! What a waste!

☩

I'll never know what David "really" thinks or feels in 2 Samuel 1. From utterly fraudulent to thoroughly sincere, I'll never be able to pinpoint on a moral grid David's response to the news of Saul and Jonathan's death.

All we have are his words and actions, and as far as the text is concerned, those details suffice to launch 2 Samuel's reader into a state of probing self-examination. To that end, David's tears notably precede his subsequent application of the Law. This observation bears up because it rests on an incontrovertible feature of the text's sequential presentation rather than on a realistic but unproveable description of the character's mind or a speculative reconstruction of "what probably happened instead." Indeed, "David seized his clothing and tore it, as did all the men with him. They mourned and they wept and they fasted until evening on account of Saul and his son Jonathan, and on account of the Lord's army and the house of Israel, because they had fallen by the sword" (2 Sam 1:11–12). Only afterwards does David return to the Amalekite's report and punishment (2 Sam 1:13–15). Lament stands out as primary within the book of 2 Samuel. Tears come first.

David not only sings a dirge for Saul and Jonathan, but he teaches his listeners to sing it for themselves—an important clue to the book's prophetic edge. 2 Samuel is a house built directly on the checkered reality of the human condition. Men and women are beautiful, aren't they? Every warrior cut from stone; every body a work of art. Every brave soldier who leaps a wall reminds David of a "gazelle" dashing over southern Judah's dewy slopes (2 Sam 1:19). In the same way, Saul and Jonathan brandished their courage and faced their enemies (2 Sam 1:21–22). But oh, men and women are ugly, too—especially when their heads have been severed and their hands have been pierced and their bodies have been hung up to be picked apart by crows (1 Sam 31:9–10). The truth at stake in David's song has less to do with what hypothetical cocktail of opportunism and grief may have coursed through his bloodstream at the time, and more to do with the crucial subject matter that his words introduce to the larger book. Gazelles are eventually torn apart by predators or scavengers, whether because the animal strays into the long grass where it shouldn't, or because it simply grows too old to outrun hunger, parasites, and disease. And as thousands of internet videos make plain, the results are never pretty. Have you ever watched a lion tear open a screaming zebra's belly and then feast upon its living bowels? This is life; this is who we are. *Idou ho anthrōpos. Hinneh ha'ish.*

The suffering that 2 Sam 1:19–27 articulates centers on the annihilation of a family—Saul's choice to cannibalize his own House. David was once a part of that family, both through marriage and through covenantal

Michelangelo, *David* (c. 1501–4)[1]

friendship. But the cement has long since dissolved, the archways have collapsed, and all the stones have crumbled into dust. It's difficult indeed to see life's lions and leopards rip apart an enemy, let alone a good friend. It's disquieting to read the book of Judges with the book of Joshua still ringing in your ears. It's hard to lose a brother or a sister to the way things really are. Yet if I can learn to mourn for Saul and Jonathan as the text instructs, then perhaps I can learn to mourn for David, too—for Uriah and for Bathsheba, for Amnon and Tamar and Absalom, for Bob and for Sara and for David and for Dan. For you, and for me. "How the mighty-men have fallen, and the weapons of war have perished!" (2 Sam 1:27). May we all be cleansed when the marble weeps.

Mark You the Floor?

Early in the summer of 1978, Billy Joel enthusiastically declared that he would "rather laugh with the sinners than cry with the saints."[2] From the outside looking in, Christian tears do indeed seem a pointless act of flagellation when in reality, life is short, the day must be seized, and fun must be had. George Herbert knew better. George Herbert knew that God conceals the solution to human sin and suffering within the sin itself. Such is the theological offense and the intellectual scandal of the Old and New Testaments, which both moralists and hedonists fail to grasp. George Herbert knew that what appears as folly from the outside looking in becomes a Pathway into joy from the inside looking out—the only kind of joy that lasts in a world beset by wars and rumors of wars. Or as C. S. Lewis put it, "If you've been up all night and cried till you have no more tears left in you—you will know that there comes in the end a sort of quietness."[3] George Herbert knew about emptiness and irony. George Herbert knew that when Death huffs and puffs, blowing dust about the checkered floor, he is all bark and no bite, all slobber and no sting. Sin does not ruin the church's architecture as one might expect. It scrubs. It scours. It sweeps.

> God conceals the solution to human sin and suffering within the sin itself.

2

An Eye for an Eye

(2 Samuel 2–4)

Sacrificed to the fallacy that war can end war.

INSCRIPTION ON THE GRAVESTONE OF ARTHUR YOUNG,
CASUALTY OF THE FIRST WORLD WAR[4]

AT FORTY-SIX YEARS OF age, I am already a dinosaur to my students but still a spring chicken to most of the parishioners at my church. The cultural references and movie quotes that once anchored my classroom discourse no longer produce an effect. I have given up entirely on *The Shawshank Redemption* and *Dead Man Walking*, let alone *The Godfather* or *Citizen Kane*. Caskets and urns disorient me, but unity candles and readings from 1 Corinthians 13 long ago became clichés. Meanwhile, the ubiquitous cultural current in which I swim encourages me to embrace the profound, theological insight that "life is good" and then to bequeath that nugget of wisdom to my peers by wearing it proudly on a ballcap purchased from a seaside five-and-dime. I am indulging in some soft ridicule, of course, but the truth is that slogan remains popular because it accurately sums up life for numerous people of my demographic: educated, middle-class, home-owning, white men. Life is good. Brooding is discouraged. Perhaps I should give in to the enchantment entirely, pull *Nighthawks* from the wall, and commit myself to the rigorous discipline of living, laughing, and loving.

An Eye for an Eye

A few years ago I ruptured my Achilles's tendon while playing a sport (basketball) I do not usually play, with a friend on his thirtieth birthday. A month or two after the boot came off, my physical therapist turned to me and said, "When I went to school for this stuff, the textbook described a typical Achilles patient. But then I graduated and began to practice, and it turns out that reality never matches what the textbook says." She leveled a finger at my chest. "Until you." Am I that predictable? Why do most Achilles injuries happen to forty-something white guys pretending to be younger than they really are? As far as I can tell, the answer must be hubris. Nothing sells a hat like a slogan advising all of us to do something again that we never should have done in the first place.

Mortality and pride. I find myself caught in an orbit around these opposing centers of gravity, like a binary star system in which a black hole feeds inexorably upon its bright and perky partner. I hope I know enough now not to overgeneralize my definition of mid-life spirituality under the presumption that it applies to all, but at least for me, a slow-motion day of reckoning unfolds at every semiannual dentist visit where I am reinformed of the gum recession from which I suffer and for which no cure exists. The doctor used to scold me like a child; now she subtly suggests to her newest hospice patient that "We don't need to think about those things quite yet." The change happened overnight, in the seams and cracks between graduate degrees. Verily, verily, I say unto you: I am middle-aged.

Now more than ever, my mind seems anchored in hindsight—that disconcerting blend of satisfaction and regret captured in songs like "My Way" and which remains crucial to the sale of new Corvettes.[5] Of Sinatra's "barbaric yawp,"[6] Sarah Vowell observes that it, "pretends to speak up for self-possession and personal vision when really, it only calls forth the temper tantrums of two-year-olds, or perhaps the last words spoken to Eva Braun."[7] I grasped this observation intellectually in my mid-twenties, when I first heard it on a rerun of *This American Life*. Now, for the first time, I feel it, ruefully, in my bones. Perhaps Bono is also correct that the old saloon singer's signature anthem eventually came across as more of an apology than a manifesto: "There were two songs in there all the time."[8] Either way, no surprise that Garth Jennings's *Sing* assigns it to the villain—a white mouse with a red sports car who gets his comeuppance in the end. It's called the Achilles for a reason.

Yes, I am middle-aged, which apparently means I can conjure up sorrow at the drop of a hat. Not that that fact denies life's overwhelming goodness. I am well fed, comfortably housed, frequently entertained, happily married, and I pop out of bed every morning before dawn to work a job I thoroughly enjoy. My two daughters launch themselves into my lap on a daily basis and cover me with kisses. "Daddy," says one, looking up at me with glassy, blue eyes, "I love you." The other curls under my chin. "Daddy," she says, in an equally wistful tone, "why is your tummy so fat?" Pinch me, I'm dreaming. Still, regrets are never far away. They bubble up especially at night, when a steady wind rocks the streetlight out front so that its dim rays flick back and forth behind the bedroom blinds. And they are not "too few to mention," despite what says the Chairman of the Board. The original sin of fratricide—brother killing brother in a world just east of Eden—has produced no personal advantage as I once imagined that it would, but has generated only poverty and heartbreak. I regret the relational wreckage, the deep furrows where the vehicle's broken plastic and twisted metal have lodged, seemingly for good. I would take back that look, that word, that sentence, that decision. Fredo betrays Michael, so Michael murders Fredo, and all the while, Sonny (like Saint Sebastian tied to a tollbooth) never stops bleeding for them both. The silent years slide by, and as our silos deepen,

Edward Hopper, *Nighthawks* (1942)[9]

I wonder how and when my siblings and I might discover the humility to confess that we have done exactly what the twentieth century willed us to do, that we have been "true to ourselves," and that we have suffered immeasurably for it. In the words of Walt—excuse me, Whit—Stillman, "What if 'thine own self' is not so good? What if it's pretty bad?"[10]

☩

The second chapter of 2 Samuel begins the story of Israel's very own War of the Roses: a protracted competition for control of the Israelite crown. When I first heard of England's Rose Wars as a boy, I imagined an economic situation similar, perhaps, to Holland's tulip mania. They turned out to be something very different: run-of-the-mill, aristocratic ambition accompanied by the usual bloodbaths and beheadings. Moreover, because I know now at least a little bit about both the biblical negative and its late-medieval copy, neither conflict's drama hangs upon its political outcome. There's a benefit of hindsight for you. Even if horseless Richard III could not have known his end from the beginning, we certainly do. The House of Lancaster finally vanquished the House of York so that Henry Tudor ascended the throne, producing (in time) the architect of my Anglican church in Saskatchewan. Likewise, we all know that the House of David finally defeated the House of Saul so that David ascended the throne—first in Hebron (2 Sam 2:1–4) and then later in Jerusalem (2 Sam 5:6–9)—producing (in time) the Architect of my church in Saskatchewan. In other words, the old, old story's rhetorical power has less to do with the discovery of its plot's development (which is known from the beginning), and more to do with the text's *prophetic discourse* through which the dog-eared tale unfolds.

All that said, it may be difficult for many readers to appreciate how the first few verses of 2 Samuel 2 could be regarded as compellingly prophetic, or indeed, as anything other than a dry and artless chronicle. David, who had been living in the Philistine town of Ziklag, asks God what to do and where to go (2 Sam 2:1). God directs him to Hebron, so David complies, along with his wives and followers (2 Sam 2:2–3). There the men of Judah anoint him king (2 Sam 2:4)—a kind of proto-coronation (see 1 Sam 16:1–13) that previews the real thing (see 2 Sam 5:1–5). As his first order of business, David sends a message to the leaders of Jabesh Gilead, praising them for burying Saul and Jonathan (whose bodies

> David shows himself to be a faithful believer, a smart and savvy politician, and a consummate man of the people. Crown him with many crowns, and this war could be over before it starts.

the Philistines had hung from the walls of Bet Shean), as well as informing them that he has assumed kingship over Judah and also suggesting that they might want to throw in their lot with his (2 Sam 2:5–7). Here at the top of the chapter, David shows himself to be a faithful believer, a smart and savvy politician, and a consummate man of the people. Crown him with many crowns, and this war could be over before it starts.

Not so fast. A different king—Ishbosheth son of Saul—ascends a different throne in a different polity to the North. The mere fact that this parallel universe exists to rival David's position in the South suddenly shrouds the story in new layers of literary prefiguration (see 1 Kings 12) and political intrigue. For the Bible does not simply dismiss Ishbosheth as an illegitimate usurper, an unalloyed villain better dead than alive. It takes him quite seriously. True, the text refrains from stating that he undergoes an anointing commensurate with David's (2 Sam 2:9), but it still grants Ishbosheth the dignity of a regnal formula: Saul's heir "was forty years old when he became king over Israel, and he reigned for two years" (2 Sam 2:10). Meanwhile, David's tenure in Hebron attracts concomitant attention and respect (2 Sam 2:11). In short, we have not one king on our hands, but two. The stage is set. York and Lancaster grease their shields and sharpen their knives behind the opening curtain, promising a hell of a show. At least we can console ourselves with the knowledge that once Henry VII established himself, England's wars finally and forever ceased.

Outright fratricide may loom large in the reader's darkened foreknowledge of the plot, but the text itself patiently measures out the beginning of 2 Samuel's "war to end all wars" in one judicious coffee spoon after another. With the monarchs safely barricaded in their respective castles, the two militaries under their commands march to battle: one led by Ishbosheth's Abner from the North, and another led by David's Joab from the South (2 Sam 2:12–13). The soldiers take up their positions on opposite sides of the Gibeon Pool (2 Sam 2:13), just as Israel and Philistia once faced each other at the Elah Valley (1 Sam 17:1–2). Then, for a brief moment, the text dangles the possibility of swift resolution before the reader's eyes. Abner suggests—if not quite a soccer match on Christmas Day—a gladiatorial substitute for full-blown war (2 Sam 2:14). A reprieve. A concentrated, localized kind of violence through which to avoid nuclear winter. Twelve men from each side rise to compete, and the whistle blows (2 Sam 2:15). Almost immediately, however, the athletes begin collapsing all over the pitch. Brothers stab brothers in the back (2 Sam 2:16), and so another of the world's oxymoronic civil wars rumbles to life like a '69 Corvette. They did it "their way."

The reader may notice that the text does not specify whose dirty trick turns the vehicle's ignition, and thus which character should attract our moral repudiation for his wicked deed. Did Abner attempt a public assassination of David's men by concealing his true intentions under a veneer of political restraint? Did Joab capitalize on Abner's hesitation to achieve an underhanded, preemptive strike? We will never know, and as far as the text is concerned, it doesn't matter. The story's point is not summed up in the question of who deserves blame, but in the fact that not a single soul who takes the field under the aegis of "entertaining" (2 Sam 2:14) his aristocratic superiors survives the match. War swallows them all, without exception. A "winner" of this contest will eventually emerge, of course, but the attrition portrayed in this opening round between Ishbosheth and David sets the latter king's overall rise to power within a crucial frame of reference: the utter insanity of war, and the fallacy that violence presents a solution to the problem it purports to address. Didn't I say that 2 Samuel would be a book about tears? Only a chapter and a half deep and the corpses are already piling up.

Numerous interpretations of 2 Samuel remain predisposed to the explication of literary and moral binaries. This hermeneutical tendency results partly from features of the text, but also (and I think, more directly) from habit. Throughout the twentieth century, numerous biblical scholars attempted to distinguish the supposedly pro-monarchic, propagandist elements of the book from the supposedly anti-monarchic elements that were layered, secondarily, onto the text's earliest compositional strata. As a result, individual passages and verses came to be seen as either praising David or criticizing David, and ne'er the twain shall meet. This reflex continues to influence conceptions of 2 Samuel's rhetoric and theology, even among those scholarly investigations that make a conscious effort to focus on the text's literary style rather than on its history of composition. For example, R. A. Carlson conceives of David in the first half of 2 Samuel as a man under blessing, but conversely, in the second half of 2 Samuel, as a man under curse.[11] David Gunn emphasizes a thematic tension between the protagonist's proclivity either to give, which tends to produce success, or to grasp, which produces disaster instead.[12] So, too, the popular Bible Project charts David's glorious rise, followed by his precipitous fall.[13]

My frustration in this matter does not amount to an academic's huffing and puffing over an inconsequential pet peeve. Such portrayals of the book's content have an important effect in the pews because they are so often fused with another, underlying, interpretive assumption more insidious than the first: that the text's theological value depends on the reader's capacity either to condone or to condemn the characters' behaviors at any point in the story. There David is blessed—he "gives" and obeys: try your best to act like David, and good will undoubtedly result. But over here, in another place, David is cursed—he "grasps" and disobeys: try your best *not* to act like David, lest a bad outcome obtain instead. The effect of such hermeneutical flat-footedness is an ethically turgid, theologically useless, rotten tomato of a read (worse than the book of Proverbs when preached by Job's three friends). As I am fond of telling my students, if the main point of the Old Testament can be boiled down to the obvious imperative that you should "be good," it could have been published at less than a hundredth of its current size.

In my view, the book of 2 Samuel certainly possesses ethical insight and value for the church, but that does not mean it preaches moralistic tripe. Or, said differently, the book may engender the reader's moral formation, but it does so not through the heavy-handed weaponization of just deserts. Rather, the book invites its reader to contemplate a web of nuanced memories shot through with theological mystery. The questions that bubble up from within its first few pages have to do with the creative mercy of God, not the precise adjudication of a character's performance at every stage along the way. Does God save in the midst of acute suffering, whether deserved or undeserved? Does God make a way out of no way? If so, how exactly does God manage to navigate the trenches, leading his people out of chronic warfare into everlasting peace? Is *lex talionis* the end of justice, or only its beginning? How does God breathe life into what is verifiably dead? Neither the book of 2 Samuel specifically nor the Old Testament in general presents a legal predicament from which Jesus Christ must later help the reader to escape. Rather, 2 Samuel advances a prophetic pattern. It sets a theological cup before me, upon a table in the presence of my enemies—a cup that the incarnate, crucified, and resurrected Son of Man, like a tall drink of water, eventually fills.

An Eye for an Eye

I am leading up to the idea that the readerly meditation prompted by 2 Samuel 2 may have less to do with the morality or immorality of its characters and more to do with the wasted lives that here begin to populate the book's tragic underworld. Following the tournament in which all twenty-four participants perish, the narrator tells us that David and Joab's forces defeated Ishbosheth and Abner's forces in the war's first battle (2 Sam 2:17). Despite this note, a glorious victory does not appear to fire the implied author's imagination. Instead, he or she seems to have in mind one of those internet videos in which a pride of lions unzips a hyperventilating zebra under a hot, African sun. Yes, the lions "win," but are we any better for having watched them make their gruesome kill? Quick like a gazelle (2 Sam 2:18; see 1:19), says the text, Asahel brother of Joab and Abishai chases down his quarry. Abner scampers away at top speed, but not quite speedily enough. Asahel hunts him relentlessly, without deviating to the right or to the left (2 Sam 2:19)—an ironic note, perhaps, given how often this biblical idiom refers to scrupulous observation of the Law. Abner suggests that his pursuer should alter course; Asahel refuses (2 Sam 2:21). "Why should I strike you down?" asks Abner. "How could I ever look your brother Joab in the eye?" (2 Sam 2:22). These questions ring out like prophetic church bells in a world where Henry V's "Once more into the breach, dear friends!"[14] has become synonymous with glory, honor, and respect. Does anyone these days remember how the English king followed up his stirring appeal? "But when the blast of war blows in our ears, / Then imitate the action of the tiger."[15] It's not about who wins the war, but what the war does to the people who wage it. We all become a little less human in the end.

Abner rams his spear through Asahel's abdomen—so violently that it pops out of Asahel's back (2 Sam 2:23). I am guessing that the sensation radically curtailed his gazelle-like speed, more or less on the spot. If the book of 1 Samuel traces out a series of beheadings—Dagon, Goliath, and Saul—2 Samuel threads together an equally horrific tapestry of fatal stabbings, of which the chapter's twenty-four athletes and Asahel are only the first. It doesn't get any more "real" than a spear plunged through one's gut or a set of railroad spikes driven through one's heels and wrists. As Joab's army begins to rubberneck the bloodbath before their eyes (2 Sam 2:23), so too should the reader pause and ponder. Let us carefully consider

> It's not about who wins the war, but what the war does to the people who wage it. We all become a little less human in the end.

what we see on the page before we throw our souls, one by one, into the grave's barbaric yawp.

As Abner regroups under a setting sun, Joab prepares for an uphill assault (2 Sam 2:24–25). But before the growing darkness can swallow every last man on the page, Abner has a little more to say. His rhetorical questions again ring out like bells in a world given to the cannibalization of its daughters and sons. "Will the sword devour forever?" he asks. "Don't you know that only bitterness will come about in the end? How long will you refrain from telling the people to turn back from pursuing their brothers?" (2 Sam 2:26). For unstated reasons, Joab agrees to a temporary truce (2 Sam 2:27–28). It's a chance to sing a carol, to decorate a tree, and to gather up those who might otherwise suffer days of unchecked agony while stranded between the trenches. It's a chance, at least, to count up the dead (2 Sam 2:30–31). It's a chance to plot a new round of fratricide, and a fresh act of revenge.

☩

Perhaps I am guilty of superimposing contemporary anxieties onto an ancient text that articulates truth through the unapologetic language of military winners and losers. Does not "the sword devour one as well as another" (2 Sam 11:25)? Don't we live in a real world where evil must be vanquished, battles must be fought, victors must be crowned, and sometimes bodies must be crucified en route to a more perfect union? Maybe. I have never needed to fight a war; who am I to judge? I have never even discharged a firearm. But the proof is in the Christmas pudding. That is to say: the plot's theological value emerges through its form, not merely from its historical outcome. And 2 Samuel's plot proves a decidedly messy feast from beginning to end.

Some years ago I stumbled via the internet onto a famous photo of two Civil War veterans who, by 1913, had turned into old men. The former Confederate loops his arm around the Union soldier's neck. With his other hand, he grasps his northern counterpart's palm in a seeming gesture of goodwill. I do not know what to make of this paradoxical image. Is it an icon of peaceful reconciliation, as the photographer likely intended—a model of the wisdom that comes about only through age, memory, and experience? Or is it evidence of a deal cut between two entrepreneurs—the moment when an "emancipated" nation simply rebranded slavery for the benefit of white men on both sides of the political aisle? I worry it is the latter; I hope to God that it might turn out to be the former. The problem is that we cannot fight a war and then, when we are finally exhausted, simply return to our schools, our saloons, and our worship services as if no regrets worth mentioning had occurred. We change along the way; the war itself becomes our moral formation. I may never have shot a gun, but that does not mean that I, as a child of both history and culture, do not own a rifle. It does not mean that I am innocent of assassination. It does not mean that I am anything other than a self-possessed sniper, infinitely more devoted to my way than to yours.

US Library of Congress, "All Enmity Forgotten" (1913)[16]

Some unsolicited advice for every catechumen of the twentieth century, for every stereotypical Achilles patient, and for every disciple of Sinatra's anthem: Instead of wasting your Sabbath afternoon on the NFL's next blockbuster showdown between one group of husky aristocrats attempting to outmuscle another, spend a little time with Mary Gauthier's probing meditation on your enemy's humanity, brokenness, and need.[17] I love my brothers. I love my sisters. And I want to be loved in return. So how do we cut through the ledger of ancient sins? Don't forget to spend a little time with the prophetic books of 1 and 2 Samuel, too. I suspect we all could use "a little mercy now."[18]

At first glance, 2 Sam 3:1 works better as a conclusion to what precedes than as a thesis statement referring to what lies ahead: "As the war dragged on between the House of Saul and the House of David, David continued to grow stronger, while the House of Saul continued to grow weaker." Why place these words immediately prior to the birth announcements of David's sons (2 Sam 3:2–5)? Or, if 2 Sam 3:1 should indeed be read as a kind of preface, why interject these birth announcements between the chapter's introduction and its narrative explication, which does not pick up again until 2 Sam 3:6? Readers who have read before may already infer an answer. At least two of the sons mentioned here do not outlive the present book; another dies in 1 Kings 2. In this way, the whole of 2 Samuel—the overarching story of David and his sons—fits within the tragic wasteland of its second and third chapters. I suppose that all wars must eventually realize a victor in the usual sense, but all wars consume their victors just the same.

To drive home this foundational point, the implied author leads his or her reader through a dark sea of psychological gaps, undetermined motives, and moral ambiguities. The first scene in 2 Samuel 3 in particular concerns a disagreement between Ishbosheth and Abner. The northern king accuses his army captain of having had sex with Rizpah, a concubine of Saul's (2 Sam 3:7). Such an act could signal Abner's attempted usurpation of Ishbosheth's crown. Abner responds with righteous indignation—"Am I a dog's head in league with Judah?"—while also reminding Ishbosheth of his unswerving loyalty and support (2 Sam 3:8). In truth, however, this tense exchange only prompts Abner to defect (2 Sam 3:9–10)—the same course of action he had just disavowed. Moreover, he seems to know all about God's promises to David, and so he throws in his hat with the inevitable winner of a war that is gradually headed south.

Who is right? Who is wrong? Did Abner really sleep with Rizpah? Or does Ishbosheth's Saul-like paranoia foreshadow his ironic undoing? Does Abner's sudden switch of allegiance suggest a mature conscience, practical wisdom, or a calculating and duplicitous mind? What private interests and ulterior motives lurk below each character's public patina? The text refuses to answer these questions, and as a result, the reader cannot arrive at any conclusive, moral judgments. The plot simply thickens, coiling around the reader's self-possession like a python eager for its monthly rat.

As Abner plays his hand (2 Sam 3:12), the text again dangles the possibility of peace before the reader's eyes. Who knows? Perhaps Abner can somehow bridge the nation's divided heart. David responds to his offer, however, with a condition on which the whole transfer of power will depend: Abner must include David's first wife, Michal, in the deal (2 Sam 3:13). David reiterates this demand also to Ishbosheth, who strangely complies—perhaps out of sheer inability to refuse (2 Sam 3:14–15). The manufacture of a legitimate link to the House of Saul is exactly the sort of quasi-treason of which Ishbosheth appeared to accuse Abner, but now he divorces Michal from her husband, Paltiel, in order to send her off to his Judean rival. Again, who is right and who is wrong? What do the story's characters actually want, and what do they fear? What mixture of *Realpolitik* and adherence to the Law lies behind David's gambit? The reader must not attempt to answer these indecipherable questions through savvy reconstruction of historical or literary probabilities. Rather, we are invited to undergo the text's equivocation in all its providential difficulty. Astonishingly, says the implied author, the political and interpersonal mess of 2 Samuel 3 (which grows only messier by the minute) somehow manifests God's salvific plan. Biblical hope necessarily cuts a path through the human condition, like a trail between the trenches. Instead of defending David's faith or denouncing his ambition, let us take our instruction from Paltiel, and follow along in tears (2 Sam 3:16).

☩

Abner arrives in Hebron; David feeds him a meal (2 Sam 3:20). As if beating a Mennonite drum, the plot holds up before its reader a mirror in which appears the heartbreak of yet another failed truce. Abner agrees to work on David's behalf, so David offers him *shalom*—"he went away in peace" (2 Sam 3:21). At just this moment, Joab returns from a military raid, but Abner is no longer present because, the narrator repeats, "he went away in peace" (2 Sam 3:22). Joab then learns exactly what transpired in his absence, that Abner "went away in peace" (2 Sam 3:23). Three verses in a row end with the same, redundant phrase: "Peace, peace, but there is no peace" (Jer 6:14). After all, to hear Joab tell it, Abner simply "went" in the manner of leaving (2 Sam 3:24)—no sign of *shalom* appears in the mouth of the man whose brother died on the butt end of Abner's spear. If the twenty-four athletes of 2 Samuel 2 be our guide, it is not difficult to anticipate where this unseemly story might be headed.

Before getting to the gore, however, the text again forces its reader to admit that he or she cannot be certain of what is "really" going on. Abner's proposal seems to present an expedient opportunity by which David could end this war of attrition, and with a minimum of casualties on both sides, for Abner has stated that he intends to convince the Israelite leadership to shift its support away from Ishbosheth (2 Sam 3:21). This plan's success, however, depends entirely on the broker's honesty. David can trust Abner only if Abner does not harbor royal ambitions of his own. Consequently, the reader cannot judge David's actions as wise or unwise without knowing Abner's true intentions, but those intentions are precisely what the text ambiguates by refusing to clarify whether Ishbosheth's prior allegations are justified. Thus, Joab's alternative perspective on the situation cannot be dismissed out of hand: "You know that Abner came here to deceive you," he says to David, "because he is working (in so many words) as a spy" (2 Sam 3:25). Are we 100 percent sure that Joab is wrong? Lest you imagine that the wily hero of 1 Samuel could never be so fooled, consider that the book of 2 Samuel portrays David's failure to understand what the people around him conspire to accomplish as an important liability on multiple, future occasions. As Joab leaves to catch up with Abner—whose assassination has become inevitable—David "does not know" (2 Sam 3:26). These words seem to communicate David's innocence with respect to the vulgar business about to occur. In other words, he "does not know" what Joab is up to, and isn't Joab wrong about Abner, whom David rightly trusts? This conclusion appears to make the most sense, but it is not indisputable. Again, the text refuses to set the reader on high moral or epistemological ground over against the characters who populate the oily pages below. Even if David is "probably" innocent and "probably" right about Abner, the shades of doubt cultivated through the story's careful reticence make all the difference to its rhetorical function.

> The text again forces its reader to admit that he or she cannot be certain of what is "really" going on.

When you read 2 Samuel, the mirror in your hands winds up reading you. Do you dare to follow this pack of sinners and tax collectors into the valley of the shadow of death? It all happened three thousand years ago, more or less, but no one I know has managed to escape their troubling humanity since. *Idou ho anthrōpos. Hinneh ha'ish.*

When Joab finally gets his revenge, it mimics the original offense. Feigning interest in a private meeting, Joab pulls Abner aside at the city gate and then shoves a knife through his counterpart's abdomen (2 Sam 3:27)—tit for tat, eye for eye, brother's blood for brother's blood. Blink and you miss it. All remaining hope of a *Joyeux Noël* withers on the vine. At the same time, the story directs its reader's attention to the crux of the matter: not a moralistic injunction to work harder so as to avoid the tragedy slowly ripening before you (spoiler, you can't and you won't), but an invitation to ruminate carefully on 2 Samuel's prophetic mixture of Law and lament.

On one hand, David immediately declares his innocence in the matter (2 Sam 3:28). Responsibility for this new crime, he maintains, rests purely on Joab's head, and so the repercussions for Joab's bloodletting will glue themselves to Joab's family tree for generations to come (2 Sam 3:29). Indeed, most of us are still paying down our great-grandparents' debts in one way or another. The narrator then recounts how David led his people in various acts of mourning for Abner (2 Sam 3:31–35), all of which produce the desired effect: just as David did not "know" what Joab was up to in 2 Sam 3:26, all Israel likewise comes to "know" that David had nothing to do with Abner's murder (2 Sam 3:36–37). Case closed, right? On the other hand, the mere fact that David's exoneration must be asserted and proven, and that the public must be persuaded of it, hints that David may not be quite as blameless as he purports to be. Perhaps every action undertaken in 2 Samuel 3 involves an unreported wink and smile, a sort of coded understanding passed between the story's political beneficiaries. Again, the reader will never resolve this question with total confidence because of the text's peculiar, discursive style. The narrator suggestively intimates but never definitively clarifies what goes on beneath the characters' visible actions. This strategy prompts neither the reader's blind veneration of David combined with his or her unilateral condemnation of Joab, nor the ham-fisted presumption of ethical superiority over against the wicked men whose wicked deeds fill up their wicked little book. Rather, it calls forth humility, self-doubt, and moral inventory. Everything about the chapter's mode of communication encourages the reader to entertain the possibility that he or she knows less—and therefore must judge less—than he or she would like. After all, "What if 'thine own self' is not so good?"

In response to Joab's crime, David curses him with disease and violence (2 Sam 3:29), but he does not apply the same legal rigor that he applied to the Amalekite in 2 Samuel 1. Instead, he assigns ultimate responsibility to God when, at chapter's end, he expresses the hope that God will eventually "repay" (or, "*shalom*-atize") Joab with evil for evil, tooth for tooth, blood for blood (2 Sam 3:39). Is David guilty of an obvious double standard? Perhaps he disavows his army captain's sins for public effect, but simultaneously preserves a useful ally in order to reap the benefits of Joab's additional dirty work. David seems to have his *lex talionis* and eat it, too. Perhaps. But perhaps also the reader should focus more on the symbolic value of what David actually does in 2 Samuel 3 than attempt to denounce, with laughable self-assurance, the shortcomings implicit in what he doesn't. Never forget that the prophetic text is not your soapbox, but your bath.

Joab orchestrates a murder; David organizes a funeral. Is it all for show? Is it all an act? Maybe! Who knows? I can tell you with absolute certainty that I do not "know" the answer to this question—whether with respect to the text or with respect to myself. Is my faith a sham? Perhaps even David himself does not know. Genuinely or not, he chooses to carry Abner's body to the grave (2 Sam 3:31) while singing his elegy (2 Sam 3:33–34). The roses flower, the roses fade (see Ps 103:15–16; Isa 40:6–8). Thus, as David weeps (2 Sam 3:32) for the tragedy of his civil war to end all wars, he invites all baptized readers to do the same.

"You have heard that it was said, 'An eye for an eye, and a tooth for a tooth'" (Matt 5:38). When Jesus utters these words as part of his Sermon on the Mount, he does not aim to abolish the Old Testament's definition of justice, as readers sometimes imagine (see Matt 5:17–18). Jesus does not tell his audience that "the Law is bad" and so let's all move on to something different called "grace." Rather, Jesus teaches his audience what is and always was the purpose of the Law. *Lex talionis*, says Jesus, does not constitute an end in itself. The Sabbath was made for humans, not humans for the Sabbath (Mark 2:27). In fact, the Law has been framed with an explicitly prophetic goal in mind: the comprehensive transformation of the person it indicts. The Law in its canonical form engenders circumcision of the reader's heart (Deut 30:6; Jer 31:33). Hammurabi only convicts, but Moses overhauls body, mind, and soul. *Lex talionis*, says Jesus, is the beginning of justice, not its end.

Many readers of the Old Testament regard its so-called "Historical Books" as a repository of moralistic faith lessons rather than as world-inverting narrative prophecy designed to achieve the goal that Moses and his prophetic successors had in mind. Thus, when followers of Christ apply that problematic mode of interpretation to books like 1 or 2 Samuel, the results inevitably contradict Jesus's hermeneutic leadership with respect to the same literature (e.g., see Matt 12:1–8). Oughtn't we take our cues from him? Likewise, those biblical scholars who imagine that the text comprises a kind of religio-political propaganda leftover from the ancient world tend to perseverate on the matter of David's innocence or guilt, as if the text's rhetorical message cannot be grasped apart from the reader's capacity to pin down David's exact position on Moses's moral ledger every step of the way. As it turns out, however, David will be loved by God regardless of where he falls on that ledger, precisely because the text does not teach (or even encourage!) its reader to sift the wheat from the chaff or the sheep from the goats. A moralistic approach to the Former Prophets, Jesus might well have said, theologically predetermines these books' message, and in that sense, such an approach therefore constitutes a bald form of idolatry because it assumes the God-like power to assign damnation to some and salvation to others. (It also makes sublime poetry into excruciating drivel, which constitutes an aesthetic crime, to boot.) Ironically, 2 Samuel has been designed to address precisely that error—the idolatry of self-possession—inside the reader who undergoes the text by means of regular, prayerful contemplation. Give the God of 2 Samuel a chance, and that same God will do something radically mysterious both in David's world and in your own. God performs a legal miracle *through* the principle of *lex talionis*, not in spite of it. God works salvation from the inside out. God applies the Law; the Law breaks my heart; my heart hungers for the Law (Jer 31:31–34).

> Give the God of 2 Samuel a chance, and that same God will do something radically mysterious both in David's world and in your own.

One more murder must occur before David can be crowned for good; one more body must be added to the stack. One more life must be sacrificed to the great fallacy. The fine details that comprise this new twist in the yarn hint at the implied author's broader, theological interests: the Law is broken, so the Law must be applied. Only in this context does the Law begin to achieve the transformational work for which it was designed.

A pair of Benjamite brothers named Rechab and Baanah stroll into Ishbosheth's house in broad daylight. They find their king reclining on his "bed" (2 Sam 4:7)—a bed like the one on which Abner's corpse lay just a few verses prior (2 Sam 3:31). They impale the poor man—where else but through his "abdomen" (2 Sam 4:6; see 2:23; 3:37)? Not only that, but they cut off his head (2 Sam 4:7) just as the Philistines once did to Saul (1 Sam 31:9). Then, like the Amalekite of 2 Samuel 1, they carry their trophy directly to David as proof positive of their deed. "Behold the head of Ishbosheth son of Saul," they triumphantly declare, "your enemy who sought your life" like his father before him (2 Sam 4:8). In this way, Ishbosheth embodies the tragedy of his predecessors while his assassins underwrite their own executions in the process. To them, David rigorously applies the Law.

All that time spent in the desert made one thing certain: David survived never by his own hand. Rather, the providential power of God did the saving, time and time again (2 Sam 4:9). By contrast, the assassins of 2 Samuel 4 have made a grave, moral miscalculation, one that stems from a more primary, theological error. They have worshiped the idol of self-possession. They did it their way, and correspondingly, they assume that David will do it his way, too. They are dead wrong, of course—as wrong as the Amalekite of 2 Samuel 1 (2 Sam 4:10). Thus, according to the letter of the Law (e.g., see Deut 13:5), David "burns" them from the face of the earth (2 Sam 4:11). As Dagon suffered the loss of his hands (1 Sam 5:4), so Rechab and Baanah wind up similarly dismembered (2 Sam 4:12). As Saul hung from the walls of Bet Shean (1 Sam 31:10), so the fratricidal brothers wind up rotting on meat hooks beside the Hebron pool (2 Sam 4:12).

Now at last may the Law do its job. True, Ishbosheth dies on his "bed" like Abner, but he also dies (redundantly) while "lying down" on his "couch" (2 Sam 4:7; 4:11)—the carefully crafted site of David's archetypal sin against Uriah and Bathsheba (see 2 Sam 11:2, 13:5). Moreover, Ishbosheth's deathbed stands in the "inner room" (2 Sam 4:7), the same location where Amnon rapes Tamar (2 Sam 13:10), leading to Absalom's act of fratricide and rebellion, and thus to David's exilic flight from Jerusalem. In effect, this short chapter invites the reader neither to judge David's response to Rechab and Baanah, nor to invent fanciful hypotheses pertaining to the ulterior motives and political ambitions that supposedly churn below his public persona. Rather, it prepares the reader through careful word choice to contemplate an infinitely more difficult theological problem: in the name of Moses, why doesn't David eventually get what he deserves?!? *Lex talionis* supplies the prophetic scalpel, which the book of 2 Samuel administers to the reader's dysfunctional heart. The Law was made for humans, not humans for the Law. *Egō ho anthrōpos. Ani ha'ish.* I am the man, and I could use a little mercy now.

3

A Is for Achievement, D Is for Dance

(2 Samuel 5–8)

Grass withers, flowers fade, and the word of our God stands forever.

Isaiah 40:8

The latter half of the verse shown above graces both the front and back doors of the building in Saskatchewan where I came to teach the Old Testament just a few years ago: "The word of our God shall stand forever." It is not surprising to find a Bible verse on display here, for colleges and universities regularly hang out their scriptural shingles for all to see. One of my alma maters supposes itself to be a "voice crying in the wilderness" (Isa 40:3) while another reminds those students exiting its chapel doors that "If anyone is in Christ, there is a new creation" (2 Cor 5:17). Each quote befits its context, but also (by necessity, I suppose) represents only a tiny nibble of a larger, theological meal. In the case of Isa 40:8, it does not take a Bible scholar to notice that citation of only one half of that verse misses a golden opportunity to own Briercrest College's unique position on the rainfed, Canadian prairie. "Surely the people are grass" (Isa 40:7)— wouldn't these words only add to our wonder and gratitude for the various financial miracles that have kept us solvent throughout the long winters and summer droughts? Perhaps I will bring it up at a future gathering of the Faculty Senate: "The prophet's observation regarding human compost remains foundational to our institution's heritage, and I move that we overlook that fact no longer." A single verse still constitutes no more than a sound bite, but with both halves of the couplet in view, at least my students would have something to chew on—a bit of creaturely mortification in a world where pomp and circumstance usually rule the roost. Typically, the standard bearers of higher education in North America do not sign up for mottos that stress one's intrinsic dustiness or the potential for regret. Who would ever want to matriculate at a college where the harvest might fail? On the contrary, "life is good," so attend GCU's irrigated resort if you like. And by all means (such as through the acquisition of crippling debt), don't forget to live, laugh, and love along the way.

Should I prove successful in this Sisyphean quest, my colleagues and I will eventually face an additional, exegetical problem derivative of the first. "Grass withers and flowers fade," the new campus sign will read, but precisely how do these words relate to the idea that "the word of our God shall stand forever"? Unfortunately, English has trouble capturing the flexibility of the small conjunction that sits between the verse's parallel halves. Do these lines of text communicate correlation or antithesis? Are they synonyms or antonyms? The reader will likely infer that plants prove ephemeral in comparison to God's word, which does not. One entity dies, Isaiah seems to say, while the other lives. Registering this difference, translations of Isa 40:8 tend to frame the verse's second statement as an exception to, rather than an extension of, the first—grass withers, "but" the word of our God does not. Yet the conjunction in question (a single *vav* attached to the word "word") remains productively undetermined when read in Hebrew. That is, Isaiah does not force the reader to choose between a mutually exclusive sense of correspondence versus a sense of contrast, the word "but" over against the word "and." The translation process itself thrusts that decision upon us. If I simply let the Hebrew rest, without converting it to my mother tongue, the text's provocative simplicity nudges me from the theological paddock out onto the open range. Is it possible that God's word remains durable *through* rather than in spite of sin? Could it be true that grass withers "and in this way" the word of God stands forever? What would that mean, exactly? How does human error become a Pathway into Promise? As the king of my castle—a middle-aged Self brimming with the twentieth century's immodest humanism—I find myself ploughing and re-ploughing the idea that David's royal city "through justice shall be redeemed . . ." (Isa 1:27). Hope wells up from within the Law, not from without.

Worship and Waste

☩

If readers know anything about the book of 2 Samuel, they tend to know one or both of the following: God forges an unconditional friendship with David in chapter 7, and David subsequently commits a bevy of heinous crimes in chapter 11. The bizarre, theological tension between these two extremes inevitably catches the reader's attention. Rape and murder will appear in due course, but first things first. Here the Promise takes center stage, drawing the worshiper's eyes up to an elegant arch that spans the dusty, checkered floor.

In one of the Old Testament's best-known wordplays, David discloses to the prophet Nathan his intention to build a permanent "house" for God (i.e., a sanctuary or temple) in order to replace the portable tent in use since the book of Exodus (2 Sam 7:2). Nathan green-lights the idea (2 Sam 7:3), but returns the next day to tell David that God will instead make David himself into a "House" (i.e., a dynasty), blessed with everlasting favor (2 Sam 7:11–16). David's progeny will suffer the repercussions of sin, says God (2 Sam 7:14), but crucially, "My loving-kindness will never turn away from him as I turned [it] away from Saul . . ." (2 Sam 7:15). In this way, the tragedy described in the book of 1 Samuel serves as the background against which the reader might discern the plotline now in view. Saul's suicide provides a dark frame of reference through which the brilliant reds and golds of David's iconographic window shine. As a result, the reader cannot help but ask: What makes David so special? Why is he different from his doomed predecessor?

> Saul's suicide provides a dark frame of reference through which the brilliant reds and golds of David's iconographic window shine.

The answer to this question is neither virtue nor faith. The first of these two options (i.e., virtue) fails in spectacular fashion. Like a rocket succumbing to mechanical failure, David's moral record will soon crash to earth in a giant fireball of toxic gas. But what about his so-called "faith," if by that term we mean something akin to its popular definition—a murky assortment of cognitive and spiritual feelings? Notably, 2 Samuel goes out of its way to problematize its characters' hidden psychologies and motives, as I describe in the previous chapter. Just as the reader will see David act in outrageously unethical ways, thereby falsifying the hypothesis that his behavior sustains God's unconditional favor, so the reader also encounters a purportedly devoted believer acting in ways that invite us to suspect him of deep-seated duplicity, thereby casting doubt on the idea that David's rock-solid "faith" somehow compensates for his other shortcomings. The effect on modern, moralistic interpretations of 2 Samuel is predictable. Some readers, in condemning David for what he does to Bathsheba and to Uriah, will register acute frustration with God's asymmetric application of the Law to a man who remains worthy of life imprisonment without the possibility of parole. Ultimately, David just doesn't suffer like he should. Meanwhile, others will attempt to justify God's legal restraint on the grounds that David turns out to be a better person on the inside than he seems to be on the outside (see 1 Sam 16:7), and thus, his transgressions warrant forgiveness after all. On this view, God does not actually grant David any special privileges, but merely takes the whole man into account. This second attempt to reason through David's distinctiveness may strike the reader as vaguely compatible with New Testament grace, but to my nose, it still stinks of legalism. I am reminded of the missionaries who filtered through the church in which I was raised. More than one or two of them reported the following: "I told God that I would go anywhere in the world for him except the jungles of [insert tropical country here], and that's where he sent me." Such a fantastic claim sounds faith-filled indeed, radically "surrendered" to the Great Commission, but it also suggests that a bit of self-congratulatory yeast may have leavened the dough. I, too, once told God that I would do anything in the world for him except become a billionaire. Oddly, I am still waiting for the chance to prove my piety. Did those missionaries go to Peru and Botswana because God really sent them, or because they fabricated an act of devotion, the performance of which reassured them of their place on the ledger of salvation? The Book of Life is a story, not a spreadsheet.

Let me put my cards on the table. Neither virtue nor "faith" adequately explains the mystery of God's unconditional Promise to David. Both solutions described above presume, dispensationally, that the Old Testament's notion of mercy kowtows to the Law, which functions as an end in itself. On the contrary, the Law was built for humans, not humans for the Law, as both Deuteronomy and Jesus explain. David undergoes salvation not because he is "good" (who is good but God alone?), but because he is good literature designed to communicate the incalculable mercy of

> David undergoes salvation not because he is "good," but because he is good literature designed to communicate the incalculable mercy of God.

God. He is blessed for no good reason other than that being blessed sums up his prophetic purpose as words on a page, constructed to overhaul the reader's heart. In this way, David foreshadows the tall drink of water for which I thirst with every fiber of my being—not because he is lovable, inside or out, but because he is loved. Good God!—give me *that*.

☩

The Davidic Promise's theological contribution to the book of 2 Samuel is best appreciated in context, as a distinctive memory appearing within a larger, literary collage. Specifically, it is framed by a record of David's administrative, military, and dynastic accomplishments, both in 2 Samuel 5 and in 2 Samuel 8. Even if this record does not read as a salacious page-turner on par with 2 Samuel 11, it nevertheless remains important to the overarching storyline, just as leaden cames bind stained-glass panels into a unified whole. And the impression that emerges from this material is one of Achievement with an uppercase A, stitched onto David's scarlet robe for all to see: unbroken, unmitigated, unapologetic success at every turn.

Point one: David undergoes anointing for the third time and coronation for the second, with the full support of God's people behind him (2 Sam 5:1–3). The narrator likewise grants him the honor of a forty-year reign (2 Sam 5:4–5), a symbolically large, whole number of which nearly anyone would be envious, especially Richard III. No doubt about it—David becomes Israel's king for good.

Point two: Whatever the scoffers may say, David does the impossible by capturing the Jebusite fortress of Jerusalem (2 Sam 5:6–8). Guided by God (2 Sam 5:10), he then makes Jerusalem into the nation's new capital city, reinforcing it and enlarging it with new construction projects to benefit the people (2 Sam 5:9–12). No doubt about it—David becomes a royal architect and castle builder for good.

Point three: As the physical roof over his head takes shape, David's biological House likewise grows by leaps and bounds (2 Sam 5:13–15). Some readers may chafe at his plural wives, but hey, that's just the way they did it back then, especially in matters of state. Every king needs a cabinet; what's wrong with a quiver-full? Even Jacob married more than one woman, and so God's chosen people were born. No doubt about it—David becomes a father for good.

Point four: When confronted with new threats from Philistia, David relies directly on God's sustaining direction and therefore wins his battles against Israel's enemies—not once, but twice before the chapter wraps up (2 Sam 5:17–25). David does not shy away from danger, while God never misses a chance to usher him on to victory. This picture remains consistent throughout 2 Samuel 8 as well, where, in addition to his battles against Philistia (2 Sam 8:1), David also tackles Moabites (2 Sam 8:2), Arameans (2 Sam 8:3–13), and Edomites (2 Sam 8:14), among others (see 2 Sam 8:12). He culls and hamstrings his adversaries (2 Sam 8:2–5), plundering and reducing them to servitude (2 Sam 8:6–8), which in turn allows Israel to flourish in the Promised Land as God always intended. "And God saved David wherever he went" (2 Sam 8:6, 8:14). No doubt about it—David becomes Israel's consummate military champion for good.

Point five: Empowered by God, David delivers both justice and righteousness to his people (2 Sam 8:15), a narratorial statement that seems to sum up the text's overall high regard for his kingship. Meanwhile, his administration hums along like a well-oiled combine (2 Sam 8:16–18). No doubt about it—David becomes an officer and a gentleman, a statesman and a CEO, for good.

Point six: Nothing mentioned on the list above survives the test of time. Not one jot; not one tittle. In the long run, a Babylonian king named Nebuchadnezzar takes away David's throne, burns down David's house, and executes David's sons (see 2 Kings 25). The monarchy ends; the city falls; the family perishes; the army loses; the administration fails. "Truly I tell you, not one stone here will be left on another; every one will be thrown down" (Matt 24:2). What are we to make of that historical bombshell, ready to detonate just sixty-three chapters down the road? Either "the deity" reneges, as some scholars say (and as their spreadsheets demand), or David's living and personal God keeps his Promise through utterly unintuitive means. Surely the people are grass.

✠

Some years ago I played a game of "Would You Rather" with my eight-year-old nephew, who had not yet grasped the concept in its entirety. "Would you rather fall off a bridge," he asked me, "or not?" "Pretty sure I know the answer to that one," I said, laughing. So let us give the game another childlike try, in his honor. Would you rather discover that Israel's holy God regards you as an idolatrous adversary or as an intimate companion? It's a question trickier than it looks. Full confession, Walter: Most of the time, I hedge my bets and split the (in)difference.

In view of David's various and sundry achievements listed above, 2 Samuel 6 explores one detail in particular: the fact that David "knows" that God approves of and supports his newly enfranchised crown (2 Sam 5:12; see 3:26). Here David famously leaps about as part of a procession of priests who carry the Ark of the Covenant into Jerusalem, where it will stay until the Babylonians haul it out again. The scene continues to inspire worship practices in the present day, but when read in context, it turns out that the overall plot has less to do with David's exemplary devotion or the legitimacy of liturgical dance than some readers may assume. Instead, the text focuses on the danger posed to humans who stand within the proximity of a divine nuclear reactor. 2 Samuel 6 traces out the Law's idea of a high-risk, high-reward friendship with the God of the Garden. Eat from one tree and you will live forever. Pluck the knowledge of good and evil for yourself, however, and you will die a thousand deaths every day for the rest of your life. You will hang up your harp; you will weep yourself dry in a foreign land (see Ps 137:1–3).

At the top of the chapter, David orchestrates the retrieval of "the Ark of God, called by the Name—the Name of the LORD of Hosts—who dwells [between] the cherubim upon it" (2 Sam 6:2). Such expressive language hints that David and his entourage may get a little more than they bargain for (see 1 Sam 4:4). Sure enough, when the ox stumbles, one of the priests steadies the Ark, and so receives a lethal dose of radiation just as if he had lifted the lid to fish out a block of plutonium (2 Sam 6:6–7; see Lev 10:1–3). In response, David becomes "angry" but also "fears God" (2 Sam 6:8–9) before calling off the whole operation (2 Sam 6:10).

The image painted thus far in 2 Samuel 6 does not obviously amount to one of great faith, but at the same time, it also does not leverage against David an unequivocal critique. Israel's new king appears to respect God ("fear of the LORD" is usually a good thing in biblical literature), but he likewise makes no inquiries regarding the Ark's proper location, in contrast to how he often approaches a new military venture (see 2 Sam 5:19). Does David finally get the ball rolling again because he loves God so much that he just can't stay away, or because he recognizes the advantage that nuclear power would lend to his imperial ambitions (2 Sam 6:11–12)? In fact, the reader has no idea how to answer this question because the text maintains its silence. That said, ambiguity in one area does not mean that the passage becomes uninterpretable on all fronts. The laconic Old Testament regularly puts a human being at center stage even while its true Subject works from behind a thick, tabernacle curtain. Only that Subject can accomplish the transformational purpose for which the prophetic text was built.

The God of 2 Samuel 6 is good, but also undomesticated and undomesticatable—neither a hunk of fine-grained cedar nor a pillar of chiseled, white stone. What's a person to do when he or she realizes that the Tree of Life withered ages ago, and that the idolatrous fruit of "knowing" has already been seized and swallowed? How should a colossal sinner like you or me respond when we run up against the terrifying reality of a truly perfect God? Regardless of how one may feel on any given Sunday morning (which is irrelevant), and regardless of how pure (or more likely, how thoroughly impure) one's motives may be, the text's answer to this question is nothing short of dance: gloves-off, hair-down, full-bodied worship. Before the priests who carry the Ark walk seven steps, David sacrifices a bull (2 Sam 6:13). It doesn't matter what he thought he was doing or what degree of conceit may have muddied the waters of his psyche. Psyches are always muddy. That's no surprise, and precisely the point. The worship of Israel's living God always involves risk, because worship automatically strips the human worshiper down to bare skin before God's irradiating heat. What sinner can stand in the presence of nuclear fission and survive, let alone thrive (see Isa 6:5)? I have run the numbers, and they don't look good. All calculations point to David's ruin. Pleads the author of this text, clasping the self-possessed reader firmly by both shoulders: "For the love of God, *take the risk*."

> How should a colossal sinner like you or me respond when we run up against the terrifying reality of a truly perfect God?

Visual and homiletical art tends to portray David—clothed in a linen ephod (2 Sam 6:14)—as partly or mostly naked at this point in the story, an image that plays into ideas about the sexually frustrated nature of Michal's disdain (2 Sam 6:16, 23). Such interpretations overstate the textual evidence, but either way, to worry about the exact quantity of clothing that covers David's body again misses the point. More relevant to the text's theological horizon is Michal's construal of David's behavior as public shame. Three times she uses the word "expose" (2 Sam 6:20). The same Hebrew root can also mean "exile." From Michal's perspective, David's actions conceal no possibility of redemption. By exposing himself like an "empty" or "base person" (2 Sam 6:20), David becomes such a person, little better than an exilic slave. An eye for an eye; a tooth for a tooth. Likewise, the loss of Promised Land surely amounts to nothing but a dead end, for outside the Garden, grass always withers and flowers always fade. No doubt about it.

At just this point in the story, the audacity of the text's sequential organization becomes most evident. David's act of self-exposure in 2 Samuel 6—not his administrative, military, or dynastic achievements in 2 Samuel 5—becomes the foundation on which God chooses to build him into an eternal House in 2 Samuel 7: "I will become even more cursed than this," says David to Michal, "and I will become abased in my own eyes" (2 Sam 6:22). In the same way, the church triumphant comes into being through no avenue other than sober, creaturely admission: "He got up from the meal, took off his outer clothing, and wrapped a towel around his waist. After that, he poured water into a basin and began to wash his disciples' feet, drying them with the towel that was wrapped around him" (John 13:4–5). It doesn't matter if the historical David proved himself a particularly admirable or exemplary "servant king" like Jesus. Indeed, much of the time he probably didn't, as 2 Samuel 11 makes clear. Regardless, David functions as an archetypal son of Man—a long, green leaf of grass whipped back and forth in a prairie gale. He does not sidestep his human condition; he does not hedge his bets to compensate for his problematic ancestry. David takes the risk. David performs the Boogie-Woogie. You can strip him down and point the finger if you like (and nowadays many readers do), but you cannot strip naked nakedness itself. *Idou ho anthrōpos. Hinneh ha'ish.*

Along with mortality and middle-aged regret comes a concomitant desire to leave behind some kind of legacy before the final harvest has been gathered in. Ironically, regret itself makes such an edifice that much more difficult to construct, for the field out back has grown up as an untidy mixture of thistles and wheat, impossible to sift. Everything feels a little compromised, and thus, more than a little doomed.

I find myself worrying, too, that the evangelical eighteen-year-olds who populate my introductory Old Testament course every fall have never confessed a sin in their lives. I do not mean that they have never suffered shame—the church's ubiquitous guilt trips remain for many of them far too familiar indeed. I mean confession in the sense of "letting go"—the gardener's acknowledgement that the dandelions have gotten irreparably out of hand, or the addict's admission that his or her disease has become totally unmanageable. "Men were [self?]-deceivers ever," wrote Shakespeare—"One foot in sea, and one on shore / To one thing constant never."[19] I would like to imagine that while he may have been right about others, he was wrong about me, but I suppose that argument would only prove his point. It's hard to imagine a Promise surviving on an ocean of grass such as my own. How can I be sure that my life won't become a forgotten waste?

Nearly half a century outside the Garden has taught me two things: weeds are certain; harvests are not. In light of these facts, I think I had better spend more time with poetry in my remaining years, lest the wars and chores that presently seem so crucial bear out as fool's errands in the end. I will pause long enough to recite a psalm. I will study a daisy. I will sing a dirge. I will streak the nave to be buried in the chancel. I will do the Twist, and I will teach my students to do the same.

☩

"Are you the man who will build a house for my name?" (2 Sam 7:5). God's rhetorical question demands a negative reply, of course. David is emphatically not the Bible's great temple builder; that task belongs to his son, Solomon. Thus, the chapter could stop right there if it wanted to, with a brief nod to whatever Davidic achievements come next. Instead, the reader finds him- or herself awash in the prophetically counterintuitive nature of biblical rejection—a divine veto executed from the inside out. Somehow, God's hard "no" becomes David's rock-solid "yes," an eternal dance performed at sunrise and again at sunset, every day for the rest of his life.

> God's hard "no" becomes David's rock-solid "yes."

God begins with a history lesson: no house of cedar needed, no fixed foundation required (2 Sam 7:6–7). A permanent sanctuary adds nothing to God's divine status, his glorious reputation, or his incontrovertible power, for these attributes have already been written into the story of the Law. God is God; no more proof needed. Likewise, the deep well of creativity through which God addresses the problem of human sin has already been revealed in both the Law and its aftermath. As Israel spirals into idolatry, God nonetheless threads a salvific pattern into his people's theological

Worship and Waste

nightmare. And when Israel finally asks for a king in order to fix its chronic disease, God explains to Samuel that the people's request amounts to just another form of an old, old problem, as old as the Garden (1 Sam 8:7-8). Astonishingly, however, God goes along for the ride. God works a redemptive miracle from within Israel's addiction. God plucks David from the sheepfold; God makes him into a military champion; God gives the Promised Land to his people all over again (2 Sam 7:8-10). In other words, the story of the Law and the Prophets is the story of God doing something totally unexpected *through* human failure. It is not the story of humanity pulling itself up by its collective bootstraps. Neither is it the story of God doing something good in spite of human shortcomings. It is a story about soil—an unquantifiable transformation of Israel's body, mind, and heart, accomplished by God from the inside of the compost pile, out.

David's kingship therefore drops into Israel's memory like a new movement added to an orchestra's already complex score. His reign comprises perhaps the most satisfying crescendo yet, like the basses' "King of Kings, and Lord of Lords" that anchors the sopranos' staircase ascent to the rumbling, church floor.[20] He is a narrow gate through which the vast symphony of Old Testament theology must follow. He is a new Adam through which to ponder the human predicament and to witness the mystery of biblical hope.

David won't build God's house as he intends; David will *become* God's House as *God* intends (2 Sam 7:11). And what is the nature of this grand edifice, this magnificent cathedral that stands a hundred times wider and a thousand times taller than St. Peter's Basilica? On its cracked cornerstone God engraves a prophecy of unavoidable ruin (2 Sam 7:12-14), underwritten by a Promise stronger than human sin (2 Sam 7:15-16). Oh David, David—fading flower of Jesse's tree—you are the Man (2 Sam 12:7)!

> David won't build God's house as he intends; David will become God's House as God intends.

Yes, yes, yes. That's all Christian worship really is, I think—the various and sundry ways that followers of Jesus throughout the centuries have found to say "yes" in response to God's paradoxical "yes-from-within-the-no." Yes, you are right, I am nothing but grass (2 Sam 7:18-19), and yes, you know me better than I know myself (2 Sam 7:20). Yes, you have graciously revealed yourself to me (2 Sam 7:21). Yes, your strange economy of salvation—the Red Sea crossroad that appears out of nowhere before your liberated people—is knowledge too wonderful for me, too lofty for me to attain (2 Sam 7:22–24; see Ps 139:6). So yes, by all means, make whatever you like from this pile of broken bones, this jumbled mass of rotten timbers and dead leaves (2 Sam 7:25–29). Fold all my middle-aged regret back into rich, Garden loam. Bury me under a sugar maple. Label me grade-A syrup. Let my heart become your compost; let my life become your waste.

4

Promises, Promises

(2 Samuel 10–12)

Sigh no more, ladies, sigh no more,
Men were deceivers ever;
One foot in sea, and one on shore,
To one thing constant never.
Then sigh not so,
But let them go,
And be you blithe and bonny,
Converting all your sounds of woe
Into Hey nonny, nonny.

WILLIAM SHAKESPEARE,
MUCH ADO ABOUT NOTHING

IN 1889, FRENCH ARTIST Jean-Léon Gérôme produced *Bethsabée*, an Orientalist spin on a rather tired, quasi-pornographic, medieval cliché. There are numerous reasons to dislike this painting. Gérôme's taste for exoticism appropriates and whitewashes the foreign, female body. He also places Bathsheba "on the roof," when the text states only that David saw her from *his* position "on the roof" (2 Sam 11:2).[21] She therefore becomes an exhibitionist—perhaps even the initiator of their consensual dalliance—rather than a rape survivor who suffers an aristocrat's uninhibited greed. Meanwhile, the male viewer, whose flickering eyes inevitably settle on Bathsheba's exposed hips and breast, may very well leave the gallery (or webpage) with the distinct impression that David's problem begins and ends with his sex drive rather than with the murderous cover-up upon which the biblical story actually focuses. After all, isn't she primarily to blame for leading him astray? So too should every modern-day Bathsheba remember to wear plenty of clothes.

Jean-Léon Gérôme, *Bethsabée* (1889)[22]

Gérôme may have excelled in the execution of his artistic techniques, but that fact does not automatically mean his depictions of biblical characters produce valuable insight on the text (a note to self). *Bethsabée* in particular entrenches several bad habits already typical of 2 Samuel 11's long history of visual exegesis, such as the tendency to sexualize and demonize biblical women. Consider, for example, Bathsheba's appearance in *The Book of the Hours of Louis XII*, which Sara Koenig cannily re-presents both on the cover and at the center(fold) of her *Bathsheba Survives*. Here Bathsheba is "explicitly and graphically naked—even to the level that details of her genitals are visible underwater," while the artist's choice to put a cat on the fountain associates her with prostitution.[23]

Her coy, sly expression coaxes David from the balcony to the bath, while Uriah (consistent with Gérôme's interpretation of the story four hundred years later) makes no appearance on the hills beyond. Even if he did, what heterosexual man would bother to look anywhere other than at the female subject's alluring, full-frontal curves? Thus the illustration's fraught background carves out all the space my brain needs to run amok. For good reason, perhaps, did Erasmus suspect a less-than-honorable motive fueling the production of such images: "Why is it necessary to depict in the churches . . . David looking from a window at Bathsheba and luring her into adultery? . . . [W]hen it comes to the depiction of females how much naughtiness is there admixed by the artists?"[24]

Jean Bourdichon, *Bathsheba Bathing* (c. 1498–99)[25]

Promises, Promises

Nevertheless, even if Erasmus is at least partly right, and even if we should certainly fling aside the nineteenth century's racist sexism and sexist racism, I still find in these problematic pictures one persistent reason not to look away: David always shows up. The scene depends on him. Without that shrouded, faceless figure always lurking in the upper lefthand corner of the trope, the sexualized female body in the foreground reads as just another *Birth of Venus*, a well-heeled excuse to go(o)ggle a naked lady in the basement of one's bachelor pad. The sacral legitimacy of Gérôme's subject matter, and thus the painting's only defense against Justice Stewart's definition of pornography, requires it to include Israel's archetypal murderer-king every time. In other words, *David* makes this a picture of the biblical Bathsheba, specifically, and not just another nameless concoction of the male hypothalamus. Meanwhile, Bathsheba—the daughter of Eliam and the already-married wife of Uriah the Hittite (2 Sam 11:3; see Matt 1:6)—converts an otherwise sexy, rooftop spa into an uncomfortably incisive self-exam. Would Pornhub do quite as much business if every video required the user to open a mirror in the upper lefthand corner of the screen, or if its legal terms demanded that every consumer aim a GoPro at his own body and bed? Given where 2 Samuel's plot is headed, I am already feeling the need for a little mercy now. *Ani ha'ish*. Bathsheba beckons me from my balcony soapbox, down into her prophetic bath.

God's Promise to David in 2 Samuel 7 expresses a theological obscenity scandalous to both conservative and liberal moralists alike—any reader for whom the Law functions as a god in itself. The king's House will undergo reproof when he and his children do wrong (2 Sam 7:14), but such correction does not amount to anything like absolute condemnation (2 Sam 7:15–16). So why doesn't David get what he deserves? Why doesn't his disobedience precipitate his doom? Why doesn't exile eventuate the end?

Expressed in Hebrew, exile is a kind of exposure, and exposure underpins the Promise (see 2 Sam 6:20–22). Prior to the moment in which the man and woman eat the forbidden fruit, the God of the Garden chooses to become naked alongside his naked creatures. The source of all biblical hope therefore lies not in the sacrificial animals whose skins become clothes for Adam and Eve (Gen 3:21), but in God's prior choice to get intimately involved with his creation, come hell or high water. The animal skins merely manifest that decision. They do not portray a God frantically attempting to plug a leaky dyke or to wipe an unexpected virus from the computer code by which he set loose the world. God has already lain down in the human trenches. God has already made his bed at Verdun. God has already wept out his eyes at Antietam and at Gettysburg. If these statements are true, no degree of sin or depth of exile could ever thwart God's Plan-A. His "exilic" nakedness—made visible in Christ—is the deeper magic from before the dawn the time.[26] Perhaps the key question percolating below 2 Samuel's pages is not, therefore, "Why doesn't David get what he deserves?," but rather, "Why do so many readers seem to think that the Bible would make more sense if he did?" Do you really want him to? Check the mirror in the corner of the page before you decide.

> No degree of sin or depth of exile could ever thwart God's Plan-A.

✠

Virtually all commentators of 2 Samuel notice and agree that the implied author has embedded the story of David's sin as described in chapter 11 and its outcome in chapter 12 within an account of his military engagements against the Ammonites (see 2 Sam 10:1–19, 12:26–31). In this way, the battle reports both preceding and succeeding the more enthusiastically painted texts in between provide a useful literary lens through which a reader like myself might contemplate that rotten something in the state of Danmark back home. Two important features of this context stand out.

The first is success. Throughout the books of 1 and 2 Samuel, David always wins his battles no matter how unfavorable the odds. In this case, the Ammonites prepare for war with a swollen force of thirty-three thousand mercenaries (2 Sam 10:6), and although Israel's contrasting tally goes unreported, we can assume that Joab and Abishai face a serious challenge. Certainly the dynamic duo must deal with their adversaries on two fronts at once (2 Sam 10:9–10). Eventually Hadadezer makes a reappearance (2 Sam 10:16; see 8:3–8), David rides forth from Jerusalem (2 Sam 10:17), and the outcome is "peace, peace" where there was no peace before (2 Sam 10:19; cf. 3:21–23, Jer 6:14). Likewise, on the reverse side of David's wrongdoing and its immediate effects, Joab's men capture the Ammonite city of Rabbah (2 Sam 12:26) while David again rides forth to victory (2 Sam 12:29–30). As in 2 Samuel 5, the good king's achievements continue to pile up (2 Sam 12:31).

The fact that military triumph frames David's chief sin suggests that a simple dichotomy between his "rise" versus his hypothetical "fall," a state of blessing because of obedience juxtaposed against a state of cursing because of disobedience, does not adequately sum up the theological nuance of 2 Samuel's plot. Rather, sin and salvation remain tightly intertwined (admixed?) throughout this book, as if chemically bonded or even elementally fused. With this observation in mind, the reader may also notice, secondly, that the rationale for David's pursuit of additional success in chapters 10 and 12 (that is, his reason for chasing down victories beyond what he already won in chapters 5 and 8) comes about through a series of events having to do with exposure and public shame. The episode begins innocuously enough. David sends a delegation to Hanun, the new king of Ammon, to offer condolences for the death of his father (2 Sam 10:2). Hanun, however, infers a ruse (2 Sam 10:3). He shaves off the delegation members' beards, snips their clothing where it matters most, and sends them all home in disgrace (2 Sam 10:4–5). As a result, the political situation between Israel and Ammon rapidly deteriorates into full-blown war (2 Sam 10:6–7). Why should 2 Samuel bother to include this weirdly entertaining vignette? No doubt the bare-bottomed entourage will titillate young Sunday schoolers everywhere, for details such as these do not readily fit within the teacher's moral warehouse—itself a clue that the story preaches a truth beyond that of a neat imperative to "apply" the text through analogy. The point is this: David's sin in 2 Samuel 11 finds a toehold in the wars and chores of 2 Samuel 10 and 12, while those military accomplishments spill forth, in turn, from yet another, wry, unexposited, and ironic moment of biblical nudity. If exile and exposure define David's Punishment, but exile and exposure *also* underpin God's Promise, does a strict, categorical distinction between sin and salvation anymore obtain? David does not thrive under

> If exile and exposure define David's Punishment, but exile and exposure also underpin God's Promise, does a strict, categorical distinction between sin and salvation anymore obtain?

blessing in the first part of 2 Samuel only to unravel because of a curse in the book's second half. In fact, David never succumbs to a curse in the book of 2 Samuel or anywhere else in the Book of Life. Rather, he remains a grade-A sinner from one end of the story to the other, and thus his salvation everywhere depends upon a God who has already chosen shell shock, trench foot, disability, and death—even before the war begins. David's Savior is David's Son (see 2 Sam 7:12–16).

Instead of placing sex just offstage so that it might point through itself to something more (*à la* the Song of Solomon), pornography bares everything in excruciating detail. Saturating the senses, it converts the viewer into a soulless ejaculation machine. From one perspective, it is easy to criticize 2 Samuel 11's history of visual exegesis for indulging the male reader's predilections along these lines. By doing precisely that, however, Gérôme's *Bethsabée* underscores a key dimension of David's sin: the reductive objectification of his fellow human being. The image may indeed suit a gentleman's club or a brothel somewhat better than it suits a chapel, but in a backhanded sort of way, Gérôme therefore notices that the biblical tale was really about sororicide and fratricide all along. Whenever one vacates another person's creaturely worth by means of pornographic gratification, religious fanaticism, nationalistic zeal, secular dogma, or any other form of idolatry close at hand, murder invariably results.

Our species demonstrates a seemingly unquenchable thirst for all those silver ephods and golden calves listed above. One demon in particular—an irrepressibly narcissistic Snake—always seems to be hiding in the prairie grasses at my feet. He pricks up his ears at the catcalls printed on every cover of Oprah's eponymous, grocery-aisle magazine. "You" are fantastic. "You" deserve a treat. "You" should name it and claim it. Always remember, and never doubt, that "you" are doing just fine. As I gradually exchange the ideological stridency of my twenties for the quieter repose of midlife sobriety, I find myself less vexed by the -isms "out there" while growing more and more troubled by the primary -ism that still lays its parasitic eggs in my chest, even now after all these years. Am I really as awesome as the taglines claim? Surely the fact that our culture packages such ridiculous pseudo-wisdom for mass consumption renders it glaringly bankrupt. Isn't it obvious that we have bewitched ourselves? The more "you" gaze into the looking glass, the better off you'll be. I suppose I must agree, but not in the way that either Oprah Winfrey or Joel Osteen probably intends. Whether through poetry or through narrative, the Bible's prophetic mirror uproots and destroys for the purpose of building something new (Jer 1:10). It impales and eviscerates in order to transform its reader from the inside out. To thine own self be true.

☩

The restless victor of countless biblical battles rises from his midday couch—wary, perhaps, of an assassination, of a knife thrust unexpectedly through his belly followed by a messy decapitation (2 Sam 11:2; see 4:6–7). David wanders outside and begins to pace the roof. Looking down from his exalted perch, he spies a painter's boudoir fantasy, another innominate Venus plastered onto the webpage below. No parentage. No children. No background. Definitely no strings attached. In other words, the wet female

Jean-Léon Gérôme, *La Naissance de Vénus* (1890)[27]

of his imagination-run-amok appears perfectly disposable, like a Styrofoam plate at a church potluck—clean and white in its plastic packaging, but soon just another piece of soiled trash dropped into the overflowing barrels by the door. Perfect for a man like me.

"But isn't this actually *Bathsheba*?" (2 Sam 11:3). Whatever David may have thought he saw, in reality, the woman is anything but anonymous. She has a family. She has relationships, dreams, and responsibilities. She has a background, and a name. She is a person.

She is conscientious, too. She submits her body and behavior to the Law, through ritual cleansing after her period (2 Sam 11:4). David, by contrast, submits to nothing. David greases his machine gun. One act of dehumanization breeds another—it's all just another form of war.

☩

Shalom, shalom, Uriah—tell us about *shalom* (2 Sam 11:7; see Jer 6:14). Still huffing and puffing from his journey, the disheveled soldier offers his report. Perhaps David saw a bit of himself in the Hittite's torn jacket and worn-out shoes, his red face and dirty hair. Does Bathsheba's husband guess the real reason for his unusual errand? Have any rumors preceded his audience with the king? Does David's body language give him away? The reader cannot know the answer to these questions unless the text reports on them, and of course it doesn't. "Tell me everything," says David, settling back into his chair. "Tell me everything," Uriah might have answered, his probing eyes fixed under his brow.

Questions for which readers might seek clarification abound, but the cagey text does not explain. Psychology, motives, fears, and ambitions—none of these can be assessed with certainty. Instead, the story merely juxtaposes the two, iconographic characters: one stained green; the other, red. David has impregnated Bathsheba (2 Sam 11:5). The cleverest and tidiest way to scrub away a problem like that is to ambiguate the child's true parentage by taking advantage of the pent-up soldier's battlefield deprivations. "Go down to your house and 'wash your feet,'" David commands Uriah (2 Sam 11:8), "while I stay here to wash my own, to bathe my hands with soap and water, and to sweep my footprints from your bedroom floor" (cf. John 13:6–9). Whether because of suspicion or camaraderie or some combination of the two (see 2 Sam 11:11), Uriah "lies down" at the euphemistic "entrance" (2 Sam 11:9; see 11:13)—not at the entrance of his own house, however, nor at the opening of his wife's fertile womb, but at David's palace door, that strange and scandalous portal into everlasting Promise.

Surely the reader remembers that, when given the opportunity to eliminate his enemy, the son of Jesse twice refrained. David would never dream of doing what the dusty Amalekite apparently did. Never would he take what does not belong to him. Never would he "stretch out his hand" unlawfully against his fellow human being (see 2 Sam 1:14). Certainly David, the *anthrōpos* whose personality dominates every page of the present book, wouldn't *murder*, would he?

After one more failed attempt to scrub his DNA from the crime scene (2 Sam 11:12–13), David signs off on Uriah's death warrant (2 Sam 11:14–15). "My sin is upon your head," he might well have mused (see 2 Sam 1:16) when placing the sealed scroll into his servant's hands. Thus Uriah quietly departs to become 2 Samuel's next casualty, another wasted life in a vast sea of so many others—the collateral damage of another man's sin. Surely here, in this depiction of moral turpitude, we have reached the story's tragic basement, the stagnant boiler room where the dust goes unswept for decades at a time, piling up on the cathedral's checkered floor.

☩

If David's Plan-A would conceal Bathsheba's pregnancy by reassigning it to Uriah, his Plan-B handles the husband's ardent refusal to dance by subjecting him to life-threatening danger in what should otherwise have been a straightforward, military success (2 Sam 11:15). The reader likely registers the conspicuous irony encoded within such a grotesque scheme. David murders and buries his victim *inside the Promise*. His military and administrative achievements become vehicles for his most egregious transgression of the Law! What covenantal friendship with God could ever withstand such blatant betrayal?

Dutiful Joab puts the plot into effect. But if David may have imagined a crisp and surgical strike whereby Uriah alone would suffer a quiver-full, Joab knows that war is messy business and that the arrow-pierced saint will require a less elegant clubbing to finish the job (2 Sam 11:16). Not only Uriah, but several more Mighty-Men of David's also

> David murders and buries his victim inside the Promise. His military and administrative achievements become vehicles for his most egregious transgression of the Law!

lose their humanity in the king's metastasizing cover-up (2 Sam 11:17). They are persons unnamed by the narrator, but they nevertheless have families. They have relationships, dreams, and responsibilities. They have backgrounds. And they do not deserve what they get (see 2 Sam 3:33–34). David stains his House with his brothers' and sisters' blood.

Joab, meanwhile, must offer an explanation for this undesirable twist. Speaking to his courier, he preemptively addresses the likelihood that David's anger may flare up when he learns that the Ammonites' arrows have hit more targets than anticipated (2 Sam 11:18–20). Joab's problem may be a realistic one within the story-world at hand, but the peculiar way in which he addresses that problem suggests that the text has been constructed to engender in its reader a habit of theological self-reflection rather than having been written up merely as a didactic record of the past. Joab does not chastise David for conspiring to have Uriah whacked; instead, he prepares the courier for a hypothetical scenario in which David may recall the dangers unique to a full-frontal assault on a walled city (always a feminine noun in Hebrew, by the way). Case in point: Abimelech son of Gideon, Israel's most infamous proto-king, died when an anonymous woman smashed in his head with a millstone by dropping it on him from the ramparts above, much to his Saul-like, suicidal shame (2 Sam 11:21; see Judg 9:53–54; 1 Sam 31:3–4). Should David fly off the handle talking about something like *that*, says Joab, be sure to add the following information: "Also your servant Uriah the Hittite is dead" (2 Sam 11:21). That'll cool him down for sure.

As the reader soon discovers, however, Joab's concern is moot, for the text does not depict David's reaction to the news in stages. The courier spills Joab's entire message, including the bit about Uriah, onto the page in a single utterance (2 Sam 11:22–24). In other words, the implied author has put the intertexual reference to Abimelech inside Joab's mouth primarily for the reader's benefit, not for the benefit of any text-immanent character, since Abimelech's memory does not actually wind up accruing to the plot. For you and me, however, this rhetorical device could not flag a more obvious question: Will David's House, built on a divine Promise, suffer a catastrophic collapse?

Love bade me welcome: yet my soul drew back,
Guilty of dust and sin.
But quick-eyed Love, observing me grow slack
From my first entrance in,
Drew nearer to me, sweetly questioning,
If I lacked anything.
A guest, I answered, worthy to be here:
Love said, You shall be he.
I the unkind, ungrateful? Ah my dear,
I cannot look on thee.
Love took my hand, and smiling did reply,
Who made the eyes but I?
Truth Lord, but I have marred them: let my shame
Go where it doth deserve.
And know you not, says Love, who bore the blame?
My dear, then I will serve.
You must sit down, says Love, and taste my meat:
So I did sit and eat.[28]

✠

Uriah dies at the city wall, struck down by a hailstorm of enemy missiles (2 Sam 11:17). In other words, the king's murderous Plan-B seems to work like a charm, except for the fact that "The thing David had done was evil in the Lord's eyes" (2 Sam 11:27). What happens next proves foundational not only to the immediate plotline, but to the overall book of 2 Samuel, which (the reader will recall) is a narrative canonically situated within the Former Prophets and rhetorically crafted to prompt the interior transformation described in Deuteronomy 30 and Jeremiah 31. Israel's quick-eyed God saves through prophetic indictment; his Plan-A precedes humanity's chronic failure to obey. God loves us through the Law.

Specifically, Nathan shows up with a tale to tell—a short story whose parabolic dimension emerges only after the snare has been set and its quarry's ankle, caught. As if reporting on a local grievance, he paints a picture of two individuals. One is rich; the other, poor (2 Sam 12:1). One owns many flocks and herds from which to choose; the other possesses a single lamb, which he treats like a member of the family (2 Sam 12:2–3). Nevertheless, when a dinner guest arrives, the wealthy man confiscates and slaughters the poor man's only sheep (2 Sam 12:4). Such behavior clearly transgresses the eighth commandment (see Exod 20:15; Deut 5:19), and thus Nathan's trap is perfectly designed, for no matter how David responds, the wire loop will catch. If he dismisses the case as insignificant, he reveals his lack of conscience, digging his own grave. If instead he demands justice for the victim, then he convicts himself. The question is not, "Will Nathan's parable prove effective?" but rather, "How exactly will the king react?" The perpetrator of such theft has become a "son of death," David claims, and should therefore be required to make restitution four times over (2 Sam 12:5–6; see Exod 21:37). Like most biblical sinners, David knows the Law even when he fails to obey it.

"*You* are the man!" (2 Sam 12:7). Jesse's son always was this story's *anthrōpos*, the protagonist through whom Israel's most bitter disappointments and its most ambitious hopes have been channeled. He was and is and evermore shall be a mirror for the reader's soul. You, too, are Scripture's target, sitting squarely within its prophetic crosshairs. *Attah ha'ish*. And yet you also remain a child unconditionally loved, from the top of your head to the soles of your feet (see Isa 1:6). You are welcome at George Herbert's Eucharistic feast, where Sunday in and Sunday out, the rich man's knife and fork carve up the stolen lamb. Such is the incalculable nature of the Bible's sanctifying math—the deeper mercy concealed within the principle of *lex talionis*, powered by a nuclear reactor humming away behind the tabernacle's curtain. Will your eyes see? Will your ears hear? Will your heart break on these jagged shores, on these ragged words?

"So now," says God through Nathan, "the sword will never turn aside from your House—forever—because you despised me by taking the wife of Uriah the Hittite to be a wife for yourself" (2 Sam 12:10). Through this statement, a second "forever" takes hold of the text, and so creates a pair of diametrically opposed certainties that appear, on their surfaces, to foreshadow two totally antithetical futures. David's House will stand forever (2 Sam 7:15–16), and yet, David's House will also self-destruct (2 Sam 12:10–11). Does the latter truth override the former? Will God eventually renege? If not, why not?

Bedroom pleasures, veiled hospitality, ulterior motives, and coded transmissions all amount to a conspiracy worth painting. Despite David's efforts to clear his browser history and to erase his hard drive, prophecy stores a copy of the damning evidence every time. Nathan points a searchlight at the sort of person David really is. Thus the king, however loved, must anticipate a day when a member of his own family will dehumanize him just as thoroughly as he dehumanized Bathsheba and Uriah: body for body, lamb for lamb, tooth for tooth (2 Sam 12:11). God will bring it all to the public's rapt attention (2 Sam 12:12). So what underlying paradox might keep the Promise of 2 Samuel 7 intact while the Punishment runs its course? If prophetic judgment is like nuclear fission, which blasts apart David's retinas with such brilliance that he will never see again, what hope could a disabled, blind man possibly maintain (see 2 Sam 5:8)? Against every human intuition, it is precisely *through exile* that God's people transform into the emplaced priests they were meant to be (Deut 30:1–6; see Exod 19:5–6). "A"s are for Achievement, and "D"s are for Dance, but it's the "F"s that finally set us Free.

Like Adam and Eve, I looked and I plucked and I ate. I slaughtered the lamb; I failed the course. I considered other persons' lives less important than the gratification of my own desires. *Egō ho anthrōpos. Ani ha'ish.* "'Woe is me!' I cried—'I am ruined!'" (Isa 6:5). And yet, much to my surprise, the God of the Garden gently "took my hand, and smiling did reply: 'Who made the eyes but I?'"

☩

"But I have marred them," every David must admit, a confession to which biblical prophecy issues the following rejoinder: "The LORD has 'crossed out' your sin; you will not die" (2 Sam 12:13). In Hebrew, the crucial verb through which Nathan delivers this good news does not mean "ignore," as if God had simply decided to grade David's performance on a curve. Rather, it means something more like "pass through," as when a person "passes through" and therefore leaves behind the Promised Land (see 2 Samuel 15–16). Make no mistake: David's Punishment thoroughly penetrates God's Promise, but at the same time, God's Promise still governs the execution of his Punishment. The two "forevers" of 2 Samuel are forever mixed; this salvation story runs unavoidably through

> David's Punishment thoroughly penetrates God's Promise, but at the same time, God's Promise still governs the execution of his Punishment. The two "forevers" of 2 Samuel are forever mixed.

Babylon. The soul-restoring crossroad to which Nathan refers is a boulevard lined with tears.

When the newborn prince becomes sick, David does not respond as his courtiers expect. As if the child were already dead, he undertakes a fast while prostrating himself before God (2 Sam 12:16). "Eat, eat," whisper the nervous voices around him, but David swats them away like flies (2 Sam 12:17). Only when the boy has actually died (2 Sam 12:18–19) does David regain his composure and settle down for a proper meal (2 Sam 12:20). Upset with their king's inversion of the traditional mourning process, the courtiers demand an explanation (2 Sam 12:21). David answers: "I wasn't mourning; I was begging" (2 Sam 12:22–23). When you ask for something different from what God has in store, and when you finally get an answer, and when the Promise really does lead through a crossroad full of pits and valleys, a strange peace takes over where there was no peace before. Again, I think of Lucy and the dead Lion: "If you've been up all night and cried till you have no more tears left in you—you will know that there comes in the end a sort of quietness."[29] The sword is coming, and David seems to know it. Better to lean in and to pass through than to kick against the goads (see Acts 26:14).

☩

To my three siblings, who were raised like me by a pair of off-the-charts, Myers-Briggs "J"s, and who remain unlikely to read this paragraph anytime short of the eschaton, I wish only to mention that in my present mode of middle-aged contemplation, I have discovered an ironic appreciation for the fact that we all grew up together on a street called "Kings-bury." Will George and Barbara's small troupe of self-possessed Wise Men risk the long journey home, from the grave to the cradle, before it's too late? Most of the time it feels like "the road back to you"[30] just isn't in the cards.

I write these paragraphs on the cusp of a family reunion. How the decades flew by! All my siblings will be there, with their spouses and kids. There will be laughter, games, and chatty updates amid our deeply disparate experiences and temporarily muted worldviews. We'll regret, but we won't confess. We'll remember, but we won't apologize. We'll hope for something different next time, but we won't do the hard work that "something different" requires of us in the months and years between. Does every extended family need Desmond Tutu as much as mine?

At some point, my father's dynasty will gather for a portrait and a meal, just like old times. Such occasions always involve a complex menu of sweet bread and bitter herbs—two "forevers" caught in the tines of every forkful. I see no alternative but to lean into the dysfunction and to pass through. So I will take my place at the table, in the presence of my enemies. I will pour a tall glass of water. I will beg, privately, for a miracle. I will sit. I will cry. I will eat.

☩

Four Old Testament women appear in Matthew's genealogy of Christ (Matt 1:1–17): Tamar, Rahab, Ruth, and Bathsheba. Amid this passage's plethora of biblical persons, the language ascribed to Bathsheba stands apart: "David was the father of Solomon, whose mother had been Uriah's wife" (Matt 1:6). She alone is identified not by name but by narrative function—specifically, by the fact that David murdered her first husband—thus prompting Matthew's audience to consider the possibility that God enters through incarnation into the deepest thickets of Israel's exilic experience. David's Savior is David's unlikely Son.

> God enters through incarnation into the deepest thickets of Israel's exilic experience.

On one hand, when Bathsheba's child dies (2 Sam 12:18), the king's elaborate bid to troubleshoot the pregnancy goes nowhere fast. The cover-up, Uriah's murder, and the additional collateral damage all accrue to a dynastic thread that eventually amounts to nothing. The little prince—emblem of David's royal House and thus also of God's unconditional favor—lies dead in his coffin, never to rise again (2 Sam 12:23). What a massive waste of energy and effort on David's part! What a waste of parchment and of paper! What a waste of words! That's narrative prophecy for you: a thick, ironic retelling of Israel's many dead sons, carefully crafted to impale the reader's pride and to eviscerate his or her self-possession along the way.

On the other hand, the irredeemably deceased infant for whom David fasts and weeps in 2 Samuel 12 is not the only outcome to which his crimes lead. F is for Failure, but A is for Alternative, the mystery woven into the Bible's dystopian tragedy from the beginning. Bathsheba soon bears another child, whom David names *Shalom*—peace, peace, where there was no peace before (2 Sam 12:24–25). Idolatry leads inexorably to Punishment, but somehow also opens the door into Promise, precisely because God chooses to get involved and to stay involved in the sinner's mess.

Looking again at *Bethsabée*, I find myself wondering if this Orientalist pin-up is really just a colossal waste of canvas: "Whatever is true, whatever is noble, whatever is right, whatever is pure, whatever is lovely, whatever is admirable—if anything is excellent or praiseworthy—think about such things" (Phil 4:8). The story undoubtedly communicates "truth," and Bathsheba's form certainly qualifies as "lovely," but the scene nevertheless recalls everything ignoble and impure about the human condition as well. So why read and meditate upon the Bible's tragic texts? Why bother with the muck? Shouldn't we think about something cleaner and happier? Wouldn't we benefit from "staying positive" and from affirming the goodness of middle life and of middle income? Shouldn't we live, laugh, and love?

As my eyes flicker back and forth between Bathsheba's naked body and the dark figure lurking in the upper lefthand corner of the frame, I am learning to see in this (and in every other problematic depiction of Uriah's wife) a little mercy now. Here is a prophetic portrait of Mary, fully equipped with a mirror for me. Here, too, is a God who enters into the hell and heartbreak of Israel's sin in order to transform it from the inside out. For that reason especially I choose not to look away. Instead I will dig, with knife and fork, into the strange meal set before me. I will cut apart the bloody steak that Scripture serves. I will chew, swallow, and digest; I will convert its meat into muscle and bone. Yes, yes, yes.

5

Epiphany Cake

(2 Samuel 9)

"The kingdom of heaven is like treasure hidden in a field. When a man found it, he hid it again, and then in his joy went and sold all he had and bought that field."

Matthew 13:44

Archimedes is famous primarily for mathematics—and for streaking. Not that he was an exhibitionist (as far as we know). Rather, he became so absorbed in his work that upon realizing a foundational principle of hydrostatics, he leapt from his spot at the public baths and rushed excitedly through the streets of Syracuse.[31] Nothing justifies a little transgressive nudity like a Nobel-worthy breakthrough.

The scientific principle at the heart of his epiphany remains the stuff of modern textbooks, but the actual conundrum that Archimedes supposedly solved had to do with messier matters of government and gold. King Hiero II wanted to know if the smith who had made for him a votive crown (an object offered in worship to the gods) had mixed the finished product with lighter and cheaper silver. In other words, he wanted to know if his subject had paid him the respect appropriate to his aristocratic rank, or if that subject had tried to cheat him as he might cheat any commoner on the street. Archimedes already knew that density differs from material to material, and that density could be calculated for geometrically regular objects. While submerging himself in water, he noticed that it rose and spilled over the pool's edge as a result. Hence, the crown also could be submerged, its displacement recorded, its density calculated, and its material makeup ascertained. Soon King Hiero II had proof of his goldsmith's dishonesty, and presumably exercised his authority to dehumanize the poor sinner straightaway. To put a prophetic fine point on this probably fictional tale: Archimedes's discovery exposes both the thief and the tyrant for the sort of men they really are. Truth happens in the bath.

Long ago, Wise Men from the east traveled to Judea in search of the Davidic Promise, hoping to find it still intact (Matt 2:1–2). Initially these magi encountered a murderous autocrat in Jerusalem (Matt 2:3–8), but afterwards they successfully located the child—not in a "manger" (Luke 2:16) as the conflated nativities always imply, but simply "in the house," where they placed before him their lavish gifts of gold, frankincense, and myrrh (Matt 2:11). Matthew's Gospel insists that we come to know the Christ firstly as a king—*the* King to whom the Law and Prophets collectively point. If Luke begins by stressing Jesus's poverty and humility, Matthew introduces those features of his character only from within the context of Jesus's royal heritage. Both the genealogy of chapter 1 and the unalloyed metal resting at his feet in chapter 2 make this overriding dimension of his identity thoroughly conspicuous. Here is David's long-awaited heir.

While no doubt exciting for many Gospel readers to consider, Matthew's interest in Israel's long-defunct monarchy involves an equally conspicuous Achilles's heel: if Jesus is a Davidic king, then his ancestry necessarily overflows with tyrants and thieves. The whole family tree seems to sag under the weight of its countless golden calves, while the damage associated with David's self-annihilating sword lies strewn about the Old Testament narratives that the listed names recall: Solomon, Rehoboam, Ahaz, Manasseh, and Josiah's clutch of wicked sons. Does unsound architecture such as this really warrant rehabilitation? Wouldn't demolition present a more expedient and straightforward fix? How can the Savior save, if he remains the product of a condemned House? Thus, having summoned this thorny paradox to the surface, Matthew offers his solution: Jesus takes a bath.

Epiphany Cake

I suspect that the whole idea of Jesus undergoing a sacramental cleansing from sin often confuses (and perhaps even scandalizes) many well-intentioned readers. Isn't Jesus perfect? What sin would he need to confess? For this reason, it may feel less logically troublesome and more deferentially devout to follow the Baptist's lead—"You should wash me, not the reverse!" (Matt 3:14). But hear this, pious Christian: the Son of Man insists. It's the right thing right now, he says (Matt 3:15). When Jesus slips down into the water, he admits what David admitted long ago, albeit with a little help from his prophetic friend: that he is a creature endowed with limits. In the belly of the fish and in the muddy Jordan River, the Christ signs up for Israel's exilic Pathway, for public exposure before the powers of this world that always seek to take advantage of the vulnerable and to brutalize the weak. Submerging himself below the waves, he acknowledges what the text has already made clear: that his family tree, like mine, remains a grade-A mess. In other words, Israel's Savior passes through the human condition. He shares his bread with self-possessed tyrants and pours out wine for idolatrous thieves. He descends from his balcony, down into the depths of Bathsheba's bath. He streaks the nave to suss out the truth. Eureka, eureka!—I have found it, I have found it! *Idou ho anthrōpos. Hinneh ha'ish.* The salvation of God is salvation from the inside out.

> The salvation of God is salvation from the inside out.

The reader of 2 Samuel first meets Mephibosheth through a seemingly random, narratorial comment tucked into the middle of chapter 4. In the context of Abner's and Ishbosheth's murders, and thus the collapse of all remaining resistance to David's monarchic aspirations, we learn that Saul's dynasty is not totally annihilated in the process as one might expect. It turns out that Jonathan had a five-year-old son when he died in the Philistine war (see 1 Sam 31:2). This child survived but became disabled, or "crippled in his feet," because, upon hearing the bad news from Mount Gilboa, Mephibosheth's nurse picked him up, fled in haste, and then dropped him, which rendered him "lame" (2 Sam 4:4). Bad luck for the kid, and an exegetical puzzle for the reader. Why should such information appear at this precise point in the story? Why is it the right thing right now?

An answer to this question begins to emerge in the following chapter, amid the reports of David's many administrative, military, and dynastic achievements. The king aims to create a new capital centrally located between North and South. Jerusalem fits this description, but Jebusites still inhabit the city, and these non-Israelites have no intention of relinquishing their autonomy without a fight. They are equally confident that Jerusalem's natural topography and manmade defenses pose an insurmountable challenge to any would-be attackers: "Even the blind and lame could turn you away!" they say to David (2 Sam 5:6). He captures Zion anyway (2 Sam 5:7), of course, and while the next verse has become well known for its idiomatic ambiguity, the venture's outcome remains clear: because the Jebusites jeered and sneered at David with reference to the "blind and lame," the "blind and lame" are correspondingly barred from entering the temple precinct whenever that auspicious building project should begin (2 Sam 5:8). Tit for tat; body for body; tooth for tooth. David grinds down his enemies according to the Law. Even though the story's etiological point doesn't exactly square with modern notions of justice and inclusion, amid this text-world's thick symbology, the penalty fits the crime.

Meanwhile, Mephibosheth may not be blind, but he is certainly and incurably "lame" (2 Sam 4:4). A fading star behind David's blazing sun, and now also an automatic outcast from God's table, he personifies the tragic harvest that Israel's first king reaped when he failed the course (see 1 Sam 15:22–23). Mephibosheth has become a perpetual fugitive from grace, the untouchable waste product of a kingdom that could have been his, forever. It's only fair.

With this background in view, the reader encounters in 2 Samuel 9 a kind of narrative eddy, a short chapter that may feel extraneous to the book's main current, but which has been curiously (and I think, carefully) located after the book's premier expression of God's unswerving love (2 Sam 7:15–16) and prior to its premonition of the sword (2 Sam 12:10). Why doesn't David finally get what he deserves? Perhaps a small detour onto the strange sandbar that is Jonathan's crippled son can help us to discern an answer.

Yes, Mephibosheth's disenfranchisement results directly from his grandfather's punishment. At the same time, however, Mephibosheth's future is also governed by a promise, which David recalls at the top of the passage: "Is there anyone still left over from the House of Saul that I might do *ḥesed* with him, on behalf of Jonathan?" (2 Sam 9:1; see 1 Sam 20:16–17, 20:42; 2 Sam 21:7). Given that 2 Sam 4:4 has already reported on Mephibosheth's existence, an accurate reply to David's question is obviously "yes," though Mephibosheth does not immediately take the stage. First we

Epiphany Cake

meet a man named Ziba, an individual who will play a small but important role later in the book (2 Sam 9:2; see 16:1–4; 19:24–30). Ziba functions as a go-between, a filter that either clarifies or obfuscates the information David requires in order to make a good decision. He notifies David of Mephibosheth's whereabouts (2 Sam 9:3–4), and in doing so, establishes his credentials. Good old Ziba—always handy with the truth.

When Mephibosheth finally arrives at court, he self-identifies as a "dead dog" (2 Sam 9:8; see 3:8; 16:9), a political and theological reject whose physical condition embodies his ancestor's doom. The king swiftly intervenes. In view of the covenant that David made with Jonathan many years earlier, he restores Saul's entire estate—which presumably had been picked apart by squatters and opportunists—to its rightful heir (2 Sam 9:9). Not only that, but Ziba and his large family will do all the work required to make the land fruitful in perpetuity (2 Sam 9:10), while Mephibosheth eats from David's table for the rest of his life (2 Sam 9:7, 10–11), despite being "lame" (2 Sam 9:13; see 5:8). Thus the man after God's own heart opens wide his generous arms, making room for the lost.

Or does he? As numerous biblical scholars have pointed out, David's actions in 2 Samuel 9 may belie a decidedly more Machiavellian approach to the human condition: "Keep your friends close, and your enemies closer." In removing Mephibosheth from his base of operations, and by relocating him within David's immediate purview, any insurrection that the most prominent member of Saul's dynasty might launch would never get off the ground. The historical David, they say, respected nothing but power and loved no one but himself. The very idea that he showed compassion for his fiercest competitor's descendants comes across as ludicrous, fanciful, and insulting—transparent propaganda all the way down. Maybe they are right. But then again, maybe it doesn't matter. As far as the text's theological interests go, 2 Samuel 9 arouses both possibilities at once. Unable to peel back the layers of David's mind, we are therefore left to think it over for ourselves: can a Promise really transform Punishment into comedy, or must the book of 2 Samuel revert to full-blown tragedy before the final curtain falls? As Mephibosheth drinks his coffee and eats his royal cake—two "forevers" caught in every forkful—we can only watch, wonder, and wait.

> Can a Promise really transform Punishment into comedy, or must the book of 2 Samuel revert to full-blown tragedy before the final curtain falls?

My wife, who grew up as a Catholic, enjoys prodding her Presbyterian husband for his chronic failure to remember where the Christian calendar has landed on any given Sunday, especially now that we attend an Anglican church where it seems to matter. Her jibes are all in good fun. I know every hymn by heart, even as I fumble about with the Book of Alternative Services like an unbaptized tourist. Some weeks I want to stand up in the pew and issue a barbaric yawp: "My catechetical upbringing featured book studies, not saints!"—except for Calvin, of course, and always at the preacher's (i.e., my father's) discretion. As a result, I cannot help but write the present "companion" about a coherent book of the Bible rather than a cherrypicked jumble of words-out-of-context. The apple doesn't fall far from the tree.

Still, I am making a good-faith effort to pass through my newly adopted tradition's cherished archways, especially where my two daughters are concerned. Although I have no childhood memories of Epiphany, we have decided to give the day its due, complete with coffee and cake. Abigail (age six) and Susannah (age four) became instant fans of the new holiday, enthusiastic for both its high butter-and-sugar content as well as the hidden coin, which anyone (anyone!) at the table might discover at any time. As they dig into their respective desserts like a pair of starving lionesses, they simultaneously keep tabs on everyone else's penny-finding status. Did you get it, Daddy? No? What about you, Mommy? "Keep looking!" they exhort one another from opposite sides of the table—"Keep looking!" I am amused and delighted by their zeal, and only marginally concerned about the choking hazard. If the kingdom of heaven is like treasure buried in a field, why couldn't we have done this in my house while growing up?

Indeed, why does any parent replicate one dimension of his or her complicated childhood over here, but then make an effort to break new ground over there? I suspect that most families imperfectly navigate the tension between their self-annihilating swords and their need for a little mercy now. Racism, sexism, alcoholism, narcissism, anxiety, and manipulation: it's quite a load with which to be saddled. Faith, hope, love, goodness, kindness, and self-control: we've got it all. No doubt my daughters will someday recognize my faults, and my parents' faults, and my parents' parents' parents' faults, for the apple always falls near the tree. But with what measure will they ultimately judge the truth? Will they roll their eyes, or will they weep them dry until a sort of quietness takes over in the end?

Epiphany Cake

Approximately twenty years before becoming a parent, while a student at Dartmouth College in the late 1990s, I stumbled across a cassette tape of a lecture given by Richard Rohr, the prolific Franciscan priest. "Unless you find a way to see your wounds transformed," I remember hearing him say, "you will necessarily transmit them into the next generation." This observation, which I have paraphrased above as best as I can remember (and which Rohr has stressed in numerous, other, similarly-worded ways), helped me to grasp something that had been brewing in my soul but that, as a recently fledged adult, I had not yet found a way to express. Only a solution from within the human condition could address the human condition, which was my parents' condition and thus my own condition, whether I liked it or not. In listening to Rohr, I realized that I needed an organic Pathway, not an ever-more-precise theological grid by which to categorize the world. At the same time, I desperately wanted something other than the uncritical human-*ism* in which the Ivy League steeps its pupils and credulous hangers-on. I wanted to read hopeful poetry. I wanted wound-transformation. I wanted a human Savior to speak the truth to my injured, human heart.

Soon the little lionesses seated beside me have made a catastrophic mess of the table and of themselves. Before them lies the zebra, in pieces. Abigail appears to have wiped her hands on her hair instead of on her napkin; Susannah, meanwhile, has plastered gooey, cinnamon glaze across her forehead and ears like a Halloween mask. It's my fault, not theirs, for I gave both of them a bigger slice than I should have. Using a knife and fork, I carve off half of Susannah's remaining portion so as to return it to the tray. A flash of shiny copper catches her eye. "Eureka!" squeals the next generation, holding aloft the treasure for all to see. "I found it!"

While her mother and sister cheer, I lean over to kiss her soft, sticky, loveable, human cheek. "Happy Epiphany, kiddo!" I whisper in her ear. "You need a bath."

We must fast-forward to the top of chapter 16, an intertextually super-charged moment in the greater book of 2 Samuel when David "passes through" or "crosses over" the Mount of Olives during his exilic escape from Jerusalem (2 Sam 16:1; see 12:13). Behind him, the coup reaches its zenith as Absalom and his followers establish control over the city (2 Sam 15:37). David, meanwhile, makes an ironic, topographical ascent even as he tumbles into the political nadir of his reign. The eternal sword that Nathan promised (2 Sam 12:10)—the force that rips apart David's dynasty from within—has gone into hyperdrive. Tragedy seems inevitable.

> The eternal sword that Nathan promised—the force that rips apart David's dynasty from within—has gone into hyperdrive.

David's journey away from and then back toward Jerusalem on either end of his son's usurpation involves several encounters with individuals who present themselves to the king as either friends or foes. Thus, while utterly blindsided by Absalom's act of treason from within his own House, David must also adjudicate the potential for numerous, additional acts of treason from without, acts that might very well sink his ship before he and his loyalists have had a chance to drop anchor and regroup. One such cameo belongs to the estate manager and informational go-between whom David previously charged with the protection of Mephibosheth's wealth (see 2 Sam 9:10). Suddenly Ziba shows up with a load of welcome provisions, thereby signaling his allegiance and support (2 Sam 16:1–2). "But where is Mephibosheth?" asks David. "Back in Jerusalem," Ziba replies, "for he is hatching a coup of his own" (2 Sam 16:3).

Ziba may have shown himself to be a reliable source of information in the past, but does he tell the truth on this occasion? His track record speaks for itself (see 2 Sam 9:3–4), and without hard evidence to the contrary, it may be prudent to take him at his word. Yet if the reader of 2 Samuel 16 adopts a bird's-eye view of Ziba's statement, he or she may soon suspect a con. At present, all of the story's power and narrative momentum rests with Absalom, while by contrast, Mephibosheth enjoys little public support, diminished physical ability, and no viable plan. A coup? Really? Even as Absalom strolls through Zion's front door? Nevertheless, David appears to give Ziba the benefit of the doubt, divesting Mephibosheth of his property and endowing his accuser with it instead (2 Sam 16:4). Such is the fog of war, perhaps.

Fast-forward again to 2 Samuel 19, where this intriguing side-plot only thickens. Having defeated Absalom on the battlefield, the king and his entourage recross the Jordan River and begin their climb back up to Jerusalem. Tragedy has been averted, except for the fact that the royal heir was slaughtered like a pig and dumped unceremoniously into a woodland pit (2 Sam 18:17). Will God's Promise direct David's future, or will the Punishment perpetually dismantle whatever edifice David attempts to build? Another episode in the mini-saga of Mephibosheth offers additional clarity on the whole.

If in chapter 16 Ziba encounters David without Mephibosheth present for the purposes of testimony and cross-examination, here Mephibosheth encounters David in the absence of Ziba. David must therefore adjudicate a second report regarding Mephibosheth's whereabouts and activities, one that could not conflict more sharply with the original. At just this point, however, the text grants the reader an extra sliver of the truth to which David himself does not have access. Mephibosheth shows up looking a frightful mess, with dirty feet and unkempt hair. That much David can see for himself, but the God-like narrator also observes (purely for the reader's benefit) that Mephibosheth's unhygienic state of disrepair began on the very same day that his protector—i.e., David—fled the city because of Absalom (2 Sam 19:24). Such information strongly suggests (but does not explicitly state) that Mephibosheth never plotted the secondary coup of which Ziba accused him in chapter 16. David witnesses his disheveled condition, but he does not automatically know how to interpret that condition quite as well as we do.

So the king requests an explanation: "Why didn't you come with me?" (2 Sam 19:25). Mephibosheth responds by groveling before his lord, accusing Ziba of slander while reaffirming his gratitude and support for David (2 Sam 19:26–28). In other words, Ziba and Mephibosheth put forth totally antithetical reasons for Mephibosheth's failure to leave the city with David's troops. One man *must* be lying. Either Mephibosheth remained in Jerusalem because he wanted to stab David in the back (as Ziba claims), or he stayed behind only because he is lame, and certainly would never dream of throwing an "angel of God" (2 Sam 19:27) like David under the bus (as he argues for himself). The truth concealed within these competing versions of reality remains black-and-white. Only one account is accurate, even if David cannot know which is the honest man and which is the aspiring thief. Whom to believe? Due to his or her epistemological privileges over against the story's characters, the reader intuits the better option (i.e., Mephibosheth), but David must suss it out for himself. Will he choose correctly?

Maddeningly, David moves in perhaps the least satisfying direction of all: he splits the difference, dividing Saul's property evenly between the plaintiffs (2 Sam 19:29). With knife in hand, he carves Mephibosheth's cake in two—one half reserved for Promise, and one half consigned to

Punishment. Thus the dishonest man in this story (whoever he is) will definitely get much more than he should, while the honest man will get much less, though at least he won't wind up a pauper. From David's perspective, maybe imperfect justice is better than none at all. Maybe the sword contaminates the Promise, and nothing much can be done about it. Maybe that's exactly how it feels to achieve a military victory over one's own son, a sinner caught in his pride who dies with three rods driven through his beating, broken heart (2 Sam 18:14). Win or lose, it's what the war does to the people who wage it. We all become a little less merciful and a little less human in the end.

"Let Ziba take the whole thing," Mephibosheth replies effusively (2 Sam 19:30), "but certainly don't cut the living child in half!" (see 1 Kgs 3:26). Through these words, the story subtly identifies the property's "true mother," an eternally poor man who must survive on gifts. Will David recognize the truth, and the intertextual resonance at play, before it's too late? Bound within his own lifetime, how could he? Thus, instead of emending his judgment, he answers only with deafening silence before shifting to another topic entirely (2 Sam 19:31). Tale told; case closed. *Finis*. Time for everyone to move on. Time to bottle up your grief and get over the court's disappointing decision. If there's hope hidden in the Bible's prophetic tragedies, we must watch, wonder, and wait a little more.

☨

Although a passing reference to Mephibosheth appears in 2 Sam 21:7, the story of Saul's disabled heir effectively reaches its terminus in 2 Sam 19:30. As far as we know, David never initiates a follow-up inquiry into the matter. Couldn't an additional witness or two have clarified Mephibosheth's surreptitious designs? Or exposed Ziba's false accusations? No such luck. David seems to let go of the matter entirely, and so we must assume that the judgment of 2 Sam 19:29 stands throughout the duration of his kingship, which comes to an end in 1 Kings 2.

In 1 Kings 3, however, a new king sits upon Israel's throne—a son of David who has managed to survive his family's sword, one who is uniquely "beloved" (2 Sam 12:24–25) among his various and sundry brothers. These days, many scholars perseverate on Solomon's faults, insisting that this part of the Bible takes up a decidedly anti-monarchic position through its ironic indictment of monarchic abuse.[32] While providing important insight on the text in some ways, this perspective (if maintained without adequate nuance) belies a degree of anxiety regarding the ethical distance between the world of the Old Testament and that of the modern church, and consequently, cannot easily account for the theological hope built into the floorboards of David's troubled House. The dynasty will fail and fail and fail again, just like David did, and Solomon certainly presents no exception to that rule. Nevertheless, failure is not the only pattern at work within Israel's historical memory, nor, for that matter, within Matthew's genealogy. Bathsheba's son susses out the truth. Unsolvable riddles do not befuddle him. Instead, he reaches down through the Law, drawing mercy to its surface like shipwrecked gold. He preserves life in all the hidden cracks where Death, huffing and puffing like an asthma patient, thinks to spoil the room. The unlikely child of a murderer and a rape victim reigns forever (2 Sam 7:15–16).

> Bathsheba's son ... preserves life in all the hidden cracks where Death, huffing and puffing like an asthma patient, thinks to spoil the room.

Obvious parallels between David's interaction with Mephibosheth in 2 Samuel 19 and Solomon's interaction with two prostitutes in 1 Kings 3 should stop any reader in his or her tracks. Like his father, Solomon must adjudicate between fundamentally irreconcilable versions of the same event. One woman must be lying while the other must be telling the truth, for, as in the case of Ziba and Mephibosheth, the two plaintiffs make totally antithetical statements regarding the child's identity. The situation as perceived by Solomon's courtiers (as well as by the reader) therefore presents as thoroughly opaque, even while the concrete reality behind the two women's competing stories remains strictly black-and-white. One child has undoubtedly died while the other child lives. We are therefore not dealing in 1 Kings 3 with a situation akin to Schrödinger's cat. The boxes have been opened; the only problem is that no one can know which entangled furball is which. Moreover, the king's initial solution to this conundrum clearly recalls David's response to Mephibosheth in 2 Sam 19:29: "Fetch me a sword ... and carve the living child in two. Give half to one and half to the other" (1 Kgs 3:24–25). What a compromise! At first glance, "justice" such as this expresses not superior wisdom, but a deranged form of pseudo-wisdom. Previously, the equal division of property meant, again, that the dishonest man got more than he should have while the honest man got less, though at least the latter did not lose everything. In the prostitutes' case, however, similar division of a human being by means of a sword would result in an incomparably abhorrent outcome, for the true mother would wind up bereft—the very definition of injustice.

"Fetch me a sword," says Solomon (see Matt 10:34). Fetch me the Old Testament's chief symbol for the penetration of soul and spirit, joints and marrow (see Heb 4:12). As if these words impale her own womb (see Luke 2:35), the child's mother reacts just as Mephibosheth did, granting the would-be thief everything he or she desires in order to preserve her baby's life (1 Kgs 3:26). But where David says nothing and lets his dissatisfying verdict stand, Solomon pounces on the woman's all-important grief (1 Kgs 3:27). Her tears tell the truth. Suddenly, a story tumbling headfirst into atrocity flips upside down. The race car careening into fiery disaster streaks past its competition to the finish. The doomed child caught between claim and counterclaim lives again. David's Savior is David's Son.

☩

Can a Promise really transform Punishment into comedy, or must the book of 2 Samuel revert to full-blown tragedy before the final curtain falls? If you find yourself in search of an answer to this question, don't forget about Mephibosheth, for concealed within the Old Testament's prophetic tragedies lies the blueprint for Israel's crucified, incarnate King. Like a penny wrapped in sweet bread, he is found most expediently with a knife and fork. "Eureka, eureka!" cries my beautiful, disheveled, beloved child, gleefully clutching her hidden treasure. Salvation from the inside out!

6

Betrayed by a Kiss

(2 Samuel 13–16)

"The one I kiss is the man; arrest him."

Matthew 26:48

SECOND SAMUEL 13 TELLS the story of two men who go to war over a woman. Just as beautiful Bathsheba (2 Sam 11:2) begins 2 Samuel 11 as one man's wife, so too, beautiful Tamar "belongs" to her brother, Absalom (2 Sam 13:1). And in the same way that Bathsheba swiftly becomes the target of another man's desire, so Tamar's half-brother, Amnon, wants her for himself. Naturally the latter scenario does not replicate the former in every respect (they never do), but the similarities suffice to suggest that more Lawlessness will soon occur: "Unless you find a way to see your wounds transformed . . . ." The Old Testament's tyrants and thieves always become "sons of death" (2 Sam 12:5) sooner or later, for the Bible's notion of comedy is a carnival boardwalk swept off its pilings in a tide of tears. Here begins the tale of Amnon ("Trustworthiness") and Absalom ("Father of Peace"), a pair of fratricidal brothers who could not be more inaccurately named. Time to take further stock of the king's achievements and to examine in greater detail the rotten timbers of his crumbling House.

At the chapter's outset, Amnon "loves" Tamar (2 Sam 13:1). This information surprises, for by comparison, the biblical narrator never claims that David "loves" Bathsheba. He "sees" (2 Sam 11:2), "inquires after" (2 Sam 11:3), "takes," "enters," and "lies down" with her (2 Sam 11:4). Then, after the death of their infant child, he "consoles" his newest wife by "entering" and "lying down" with her again (2 Sam 12:24), but David does not "love" her in the same way that God "loves" their son, Solomon (2 Sam 12:24). As a result of this dissimilarity, the verb's appearance in 2 Sam 13:1 leaps off the page, especially for anyone who already knows what predatory sins lie crouching at Amnon's door. If the reader could ignore those sins and judge Amnon on the basis of "love" alone, he or she might be tempted (at least momentarily) to give the prince's passion the benefit of the doubt. After all, most of us have been there before, wanting someone we cannot have. But that interpretive fruit quickly dies on the vine. Additional clues that Amnon's so-called "love" expresses something very different from the real thing—that it catalyzes the transfer of evil from one generation to the next—spring up throughout the next few verses like well-watered dandelions. Thus, reading forward, any hint of Amnon's potential as a divinely favored Davidic seed akin to Solomon vanishes below the story's numerous weeds.

Previously, David "loved" Jonathan (1 Sam 20:17), and so found himself much "grieved" or "distressed" when Jonathan died (2 Sam 1:26). In the present narrative, too, the lover finds himself in corresponding "distress" (2 Sam 13:2). The reader soon learns, however, that Amnon's anguish stems not from the loss of a concrete good (such as friendship), but from frustration regarding an unrealized fantasy. His interest in Tamar renders him physically "sick" (or so he imagines) because she is an unmarried virgin, and as such, Amnon cannot envision how he might "do anything to her" (2 Sam 13:2)—as if she would be considered a legitimate target in some other (military?) situation, and as if "doing something" to another person presented a valid definition of the "love" from which he supposedly suffers. The reader may infer, therefore, that the text portrays Amnon's affection for his half-sister as a euphemism for sexual self-interest, which the rape goes on to confirm in horrifying detail. Writ large, the Old Testament knows all about the sublime world of mutually expressed eroticism, but nothing of the sort shows up in 2 Samuel 13. Amnon's world begins and ends with Amnon, and so the self-giving Song of Solomon must wait for another day.

Amnon, in other words, is no true lover. Neither is he very wise. The "wisdom" (root *ḥkm*; see 1 Kgs 3:12) of God characteristically restores doomed children to their rightful mothers (1 Kgs 3:16–28; cf. 2 Sam

19:24–30). Real wisdom preserves life. By contrast, Amnon's wisdom amounts to stagecraft, a form of artifice designed to manufacture a predetermined outcome. His buddy Jonadab is a "very smart" guy (root *ḥkm*; 2 Sam 13:3), observes the narrator, but that fact does not ensure his Ivy League education will accrue to the public good.

Once the prince reveals to Jonadab the reason for his daily doldrums (2 Sam 13:4), the straight-A student cooks up a plan. All you need to do, he says to Amnon, is "lie down" (see 2 Sam 4:5; 11:4) on your "couch" (see 2 Sam 4:5; 11:2) and pretend to be "sick" (2 Sam 13:5). When your clueless father comes for a visit, simply persuade him to have Tamar bake chocolate chip cookies for you in private, and preferably topless. As the reader soon discovers, however, the purported brilliance of this scheme applies more to Jonadab himself than to Amnon. If the prince, while perched on his voyeuristic roof, chooses to sit on his hands while Tamar sweats over the stove, then Jonadab will receive credit for having put together an alluring peepshow. Conversely, if Amnon takes advantage of the situation (as he certainly will), leading to unwanted political fallout with David and/or Absalom (see 2 Sam 13:21–22), Jonadab can always disabuse himself of these repercussions: "I never told you to rape her!" Never mind that his word choice from the beginning tosses Amnon—who is looking more and more unwise and less and less "trustworthy" by the second—onto the symbolic "recliner," one of the primary locations where biblical royalty loses its soul. As I often tell my students: if you wake up tomorrow and find yourself in the Old Testament, whatever you do, don't get "sick in bed" like Amnon (e.g., 2 Kgs 1:2–4) unless a prophet invested in your resurrection happens to have stationed himself nearby (e.g., 1 Kgs 17:19–23). In sum, the firstborn son of David dooms himself from the moment he follows his sharp friend's not-so-sharp advice (2 Sam 13:6), for Amnon's counterfeit "love" isn't really love, and his friend's bankrupt "wisdom" isn't really wisdom. The men in this excruciating chapter of the Old Testament prove ironic caricatures of the real thing,

> The firstborn son of David dooms himself from the moment he follows his sharp friend's not-so-sharp advice.

while the unfortunate person caught in between loses everything beneath their oh-so-passionate *Songs of Myself*.

Approximately fifteen years ago, I began working toward a PhD through Duke University's Graduate Program in Religion (GPR), which is sponsored both by the university's Department of Religious Studies and by its Divinity School (a seminary of the United Methodist Church). As a result of this exceptionally generative but sometimes unwieldy partnership, GPR students must often navigate the differences between an "outsider" and an "insider" approach to the study of religion. For example, not long after I arrived on campus, I attended a convocation service along with several hundred other budding graduate students who, like me, stood on the edge of an elite education in fields ranging across the sciences and humanities. The effusive speaker, I vividly recall, stood in the Chapel pulpit beneath its soaring arches and encouraged us to use our time and newly available resources to reach for the stars—in his words, to "Be awesome!" to the very best of our abilities. He stroked our accomplishments, fondled our pride, and made love to our egos. Having attained an undergraduate degree at an Ivy League institution some ten years prior, I experienced the moment as a depressing reentry into the thick fog of secular humanism. A flood of classroom memories came rushing back. Ah, yes. Collective "wisdom" supposedly deepens through the pursuit of isolated, individual achievement.

What would an education founded on the self-giving Song of Solomon look like instead? Could it heal wounds? Might it transform entrenched, intergenerational sins? Perhaps I would get an answer at the Graduate School's required "ethics" workshop where again, some months later, I sat down shoulder-to-shoulder with hundreds of my awesome peers who were only getting awesomer by the minute. The idea, I gathered, was to help the university's newest crop of young researchers navigate questions regarding plagiarism and data fraud. A worthy goal, but the lecture's delivery by an individual utterly bereft of theological education should have raised every eyebrow in the room. A *lawyer* teaching an *ethics* workshop? Seriously, Duke? At least he could help us sift our behaviors so as to avoid getting caught.

Perhaps no work of art captures my frustration with that lecture—seared into my memory for all the wrong reasons—better than Gustav Klimt's *The Kiss*. Its extravagant use of gold leaf recalls Byzantine iconography, but the "lovers" it depicts are not the Father, Son, and Holy Spirit. Rather, they are two human beings clutching one another in a strictly human embrace. If in Scripture "God is love" (1 John 4:16), Klimt's posterchild of the American university dorm turns that definition upside down. Here "love" becomes god for an uncatechized generation thoroughly unprepared to give and receive the object of their depersonalized "faith," which devolves into a legal code incapable of mercy now. Was anyone else listening to the wise workshop leader's subtext? Love simply does not happen in a world populated by the rigorously self-possessed.

Gustav Klimt, *The Kiss* (1907–8)[33]

"This is how we know what love is: Jesus Christ laid down his life for us. And we ought to lay down our lives for our brothers and sisters" (1 John 3:16). The Christian Bible's definition of love centers on a Person. Through the gift of himself, Jesus creates a Pathway through which his followers learn to do the same, thereby undergoing transformation from the inside out. For two thousand years, these followers have regularly and repeatedly proven themselves less than awesome. But is that any great surprise? The church is a hospital for sinners, not a jury of saints. Very likely the powers-that-be will never invite me to address a new generation of secular superstars, but should that opportunity arise, I will have delivered my remarks here, in advance: "Fellow worms, you can forget about 'being awesome,' because you aren't. Whatever your prior accomplishments, I encourage you to declare your intellectual and moral bankruptcy straightaway, for it's the 'F's that set us Free. Get needy. Be forgiven. And be redeemed."

After Jonadab writes the script, Amnon speedily puts his "wise" friend's advice into effect. But when the king comes to visit his "sick" son as predicted, Amnon improvises with a little extra vocabulary of his own: "Let's have my sister Tamar make 'heart-cakes,'" he says to David, "a couple of 'heart-cakes' for me to eat right out of her hand!" (2 Sam 13:6). The prince wants not just "food" from his future rape victim (see 2 Sam 13:5), but a very specific and evocative Valentine's Day treat. How charming.

As the plot's rising action drives toward Amnon's crime, it is important to remember that David remains the text's chief theological icon from beginning to end, even when 2 Samuel temporarily aims its spotlight at the supporting cast. Every scene in the book contributes in one way or another to his mysterious mixture of wasted achievements and undignified dance. So what should we make of his brief appearance in 2 Samuel 13? I suspect that for some readers, David's apparent naïveté at this stage in the plot warrants criticism, for by overindulging his son, he inadvertently throws his daughter under the bus (2 Sam 13:7). Doesn't he guess Amnon's ulterior motives? Can he really be so dense? Perhaps a father who remained in closer emotional contact with his children would not have fallen for such an obvious ruse. I doubt, however, that contemporary anxieties regarding David's theory of childrearing really provide the best angle on this ancient text. The tragic tale of Amnon, Tamar, and Absalom is less about David's failure as a parent than it paints a picture of David's helplessness, his thorough inability to outmaneuver the sword that Nathan predicted in 2 Sam 12:10. Because of what he did to Bathsheba and to Uriah, David must travel an exilic path. Thus, the primary question in view concerns the paradoxical tension between the reliability of God's Promise and the inevitability of Punishment. At least for now, the latter vector seems to have seized the upper hand, and therefore begins the task of stripping the dynasty naked and pulling its rafters down to dust.

Soon Amnon gets the culinary peep-show that Jonadab contrived. But when Tamar finally produces her "heart," the prince refuses to eat (2 Sam 13:8–9)—an ironic echo, perhaps, of the king's fast on behalf of his (verifiably) sick son in 2 Sam 12:17. Any way you slice the cake, David's archetypal sin produces dead children. Here we go again.

> The primary question in view concerns the paradoxical tension between the reliability of God's Promise and the inevitability of Punishment.

For Tamar, Amnon's lack of gastronomic appetite may seem like the "trustworthy" behavior of a very sick man indeed. But for the reader who knows all too well that Amnon is shamming, the prince's actions only underscore the potency of his sexual appetite, which he will soon satisfy whether Tamar likes it or not. But first, some ambience. Mood music. Candlelight, and all that. He draws her to his bedside in the "inner room" (2 Sam 13:10), precisely the same location where Ishbosheth, "lying down on his couch" (2 Sam 4:5), woke up to discover a sword driven through his abdomen (2 Sam 4:6–7). "Lie-down with me!" says David's son to David's daughter (2 Sam 13:11; see 11:4), and you, too, will find your belly impaled by a different kind of "sword."

Law-conscious Tamar resists, and in a way that shines the brightest possible light on Amnon's transgression. "Don't rape me!" she pleads— "Don't do this 'corpse-like' thing!" (2 Sam 13:12). "If you go through with it," she continues, "you'll become a corpse!" (2 Sam 13:13). Get it? As in, "My brother Absalom will kill you before the chapter wraps up"? Naturally this clue sails over not-so-smart Amnon's head. He rapes Tamar anyway (2 Sam 13:14), carving her body into twelve pieces with every stab of his knife (see Judg 19:29). Again, as if it were not painfully obvious already, the father's tyrannical wildfire whips through the subsequent generation, yielding dead bodies everywhere we look.

"Then Amnon hated her with a very deep hatred; indeed, the hatred with which he hated her was deeper than the 'love' with which he had loved her" (2 Sam 13:15). "Get up," said the Levite to his concubine, her silent hands clutching the threshold. "Let's go" (Judg 19:27–28). "Get up," says Amnon to the woman on whose soul he has just feasted. "Get lost" (2 Sam 13:15)—and "bolt the door behind her!" (2 Sam 13:17). Thus he ruins not only Tamar's day, but every subsequent day as well, for now she must subsist in her brother Absalom's house as a virtual widow, eternally bereft of Promise (2 Sam 13:18–20).

Whenever human beings fail to love—such as in the Old Testament's appalling memories of sororicide and fratricide—open wounds and perpetual grief fill the void. So first be redeemed; only afterwards preach your sermon. A note to convocation speakers everywhere, lest you betray your students with a kiss.

☩

Absalom, for his part, immediately guesses what David could not. "Don't take it to heart," he instructs Tamar, thus immortalizing himself as the worst therapist of all time (2 Sam 13:20). No problem, the reader may imagine Tamar thinking to herself as she rolls her eyes. I'll get right on that. Amnon kicks her out the door (2 Sam 13:17), David gets angry but takes no further action (2 Sam 13:21), and Absalom channels his outrage into "hatred" (2 Sam 13:22; see 13:15). In other words, the men of the House all focus on something other than the person who has just been destroyed. Failure to love produces failure to love produces failure to love (see Deut 5:9). Hence Nathan's sword, unimpeded by Promise, swings around for another strike.

Two years go by. Absalom invites David to a sheep-shearing festival at Baal Hazor (2 Sam 13:23–24). When the king declines, the reader gains new insight into the discrepancy between Absalom's public persona and his private machinations (see 2 Sam 13:22), a disquieting trait that defines his character as the story unfolds. Just as Amnon carved up Tamar, so Absalom's identity divides in half. He "urges" David to attend (2 Sam 13:25, 27), but as the reader suspects or knows already, the last person Absalom would really want at Baal Hazor is the king, since he will use David's absence to murder Amnon in retaliation for what Amnon did to Tamar (2 Sam 13:28; see 13:32). Amnon feigned sickness (see 2 Sam 13:6); now Absalom also hoodwinks their gullible dad. Like a ship without a mast, David founders before the next generation's relentless thirst for war. Here we go again.

When Amnon's "heart" has begun to feel its ironic best, Absalom puts his plan into effect. Acting as the arbiter of divine Law, he sends his soldiers to the front (2 Sam 13:28) to achieve "justice" for Tamar by killing her rapist. Then, having recognized what their brother is capable of doing, the other princes hop into their red Corvettes and hit the gas (2 Sam 13:29).

Where does David stand in relation to all this? As titillating as fratricide and high treason within Israel's royal family may be, and as many historical and political questions as such an assassination may raise, the text highlights the king's confusion and grief instead. Hearing an exaggerated version of the bad news, David more or less collapses (2 Sam 13:31), and then, with his remaining sons, he "weeps a very great weeping" (2 Sam 13:36). All the while, he must rely on "wise" Jonadab—the architect of Amnon's original deceit—to sort disinformation from the truth (2 Sam 13:32). In the same way that Absalom told Tamar not to set her "heart" on the violation of her body (2 Sam 13:20), so Jonadab tells David not to take any swirling rumors of a mass regicide to "heart" (2 Sam 13:33). He is forensically correct, of course, but grossly mistaken at a thematic and theological level. David's daughter has been raped and his heir (the perpetrator!) has been murdered while the heir's dynastic replacement (again, the perpetrator!!) disappears into exile (2 Sam 13:37–38). Who wouldn't cry a river over that?

☩

Imagine the disciples' confusion. Groggy from sleep, one of their own suddenly appears in the Garden with a gang of soldiers wielding swords and clubs (Matt 26:45–47). Before they can guess what is happening, Judas steps from torchlight into gloom and presses his lips gently upon Jesus's cheek. Is this an act of love? Secretly, the gesture transmits coded information to the war machine at the betrayer's back, deployed by the powers-that-be to take the Lover into custody and thereby shutter his institutional doors for good (Matt 26:48–49). With a simple kiss, Judas Iscariot discloses the primary tenet of his ethical philosophy: check the wind, read the writing on the wall, and go with the cultural flow. Calculate your data and organize your behaviors to avoid getting caught.

Jesus has little difficulty in seeing through his student's self-interest: "Do what you came for, friend" (Matt 26:50). One wonders if Judas looked him squarely in the face. More likely he averted his eyes as the soldiers threw handcuffs on Jesus from behind. Whenever I'm feeling particularly savvy, exceptionally wise, or especially awesome, it's no fun to remember that I'm not.

At this point the disciples finally seem to get the message: Jesus has been arrested. One of them draws a sword (Matt 26:51); another whips out a concealed Glock; still a third greases his AK-47, ready for the teacher's command. Just say the word, Rabbi, and a hailstorm of bullets will transform your enemies into dust. But the Lover refuses to bite. You can put away your man-toys, says Jesus (Matt 26:52), because the events about to occur, right here on Israel's rutted-out Trail of Tears, constitute the fulfillment of Old Testament prophecy (Matt 26:56). The deep distrust, the thick patterns of betrayal, the rapes, thefts, and murders, the false gods and the false testimonies, the crumbling House, and the unavoidable Punishment that rips like wildfire through one broken generation after another—all this will be addressed, says David's Son, from the inside out. All this has been and will be redeemed through love: "Jesus Christ laid down his life for us" (1 John 3:16).

☩

Absalom has fled. As a result, David's "heart" fixes upon his son (2 Sam 14:1), but the narrator does not describe any further the texture of his rumination. Should we imagine that the king grieves for Absalom as a father grieves for a prodigal child? Or does he worry more about the political threat that a disenfranchised claimant to the throne—one who has just proven himself capable of both fratricide and regicide—poses to his own safety? The text's vocabulary and syntax leave the answers to these questions ambiguous, while the overall storyline refrains (as usual) from drilling into its characters' psychologies in the same way that a modern novel would. Instead, the implied author focuses his or her reader's attention on the plot's archetypal and symbolic surface—in this case, the mechanism by which David attempts to patch his House's cracked foundation and its leaky, basement walls. The king has no interest in his dynasty's destruction; neither can he easily reinstate Absalom to his position as if Amnon's murder had never happened. So how will David address this unsolvable problem?

> The king has no interest in his dynasty's destruction; neither can he easily reinstate Absalom to his position as if Amnon's murder had never happened. So how will David address this unsolvable problem?

Chapter 14 begins by reintroducing another wise guy like Jonadab. The reader has already gotten a feel for Joab's street smarts in chapter 3, when he shoved a knife through Abner's belly, and in chapter 11, when he facilitated David's plan to murder Uriah. Here the foremost son of Zeruiah (see 2 Sam 3:39) returns to the spotlight with an elaborate plan to disentangle his master's weeds. Perhaps it is only natural that readers should want to know what motivates Joab to involve himself in David's dilemma, and scholars have tried over the years to answer this question.[34] Once again, however, the text avoids a deep dive into its characters' anxieties and ambitions. This literary fact suggests that the scene's iconographic foreground remains more important to the book's theological horizon than its fraught background. In other words, Joab's relevance to 2 Samuel 14 has less to do with whatever the general hopes to gain (and which the reader can appreciate only through a speculative reconstruction of Joab's mind), and more to do with what his record of violence and manipulation add to the present scene.

Joab's plan hinges on a smart person pretending to be something she isn't. This point should set off every alarm bell in the reader's mental fire station. Just as Amnon took his cues from "wise" Jonadab (2 Sam 13:3) by "feigning-sickness" (2 Sam 13:5–6), so also Joab directs the "wise" woman from Tekoa to "feign-mourning" in her upcoming audience with the king (2 Sam 14:2). Then, in the same way that Jonadab fed Amnon his lines, Joab explicitly "puts words into her mouth" (2 Sam 14:3). Whom to trust in a world of lies? It seems that Absalom's political limbo manifests only a symptom of David's true predicament: the king does not sail his own ship. And if Punishment has taken control of the rudder, then no amount of savvy troubleshooting will avoid a wreck. The cracks cannot be sealed; the leaks cannot be plugged.

The woman whose purported "wisdom" consists of taking orders directly from Joab sells David a story about fratricide—a Cain-and-Abel-type tale where one boy, in a fit of rage, takes his brother's life (2 Sam 14:6). The problem, she explains, turns on the fact that her husband has already died (untrue) and that her fellow villagers now want to execute her remaining son (also untrue), which would leave her without a future in the land (2 Sam 14:5, 7). At this point, the reader may register an analogical correspondence between the woman's fictional scenario and David's circumstances, even if the parallels remain inexact: two sons, rage followed by murder, and the desire to rehabilitate the guilty party. David rules on the woman's behalf (2 Sam 14:8), but does not indicate that he has connected her plight to his own, so she continues to press her point (2 Sam 14:9). When David still does not make the leap of association (2 Sam 14:10–11), the woman from Tekoa spells it out. The issue at stake has do with "calculation" (2 Sam

14:13). Human beings, she says, live unidirectional lives. They travel inexorably toward their graves, from which no return journey can be made. God, on the other hand, "calculates calculations" beyond what is normally possible so that banished persons, for example, can recover from their banishment after all (2 Sam 14:14). If David can rule rightly in her case, the woman asks, why won't he apply his God-like acuity for good and evil (2 Sam 14:17) to his own affairs (2 Sam 14:13)?

The woman's point sounds correct in the grand scheme of both the Old and New Testaments, and the canonical reader may very well want to preach something like it before all is said and done. God's strange math redeems exilic Israel from captivity and settles it once more in the Promised Land (see Isa 55:8). That the woman articulates this intertextual truth while engaged in a local fraud, however, throws the value of her theological insight into serious doubt, in the same way that Job's friends impose proverbial generalizations onto a situation where those generalizations do not actually apply. Is the tale of Amnon, Tamar, and Absalom a redemption story as the woman from Tekoa suggests? My heart desperately wants it to be—I desire transformation for this trio of troubled siblings in the same way that I long for the repair of my own parents' House. But true wisdom has nothing to do with manufacturing results; it is about accepting God's movement in the dark.

When David finally catches up to Joab's artifice (2 Sam 14:18–19), the woman from Tekoa lauds him for demonstrating "wisdom" akin to that of an "angel of God" (see 2 Sam 14:17) and for "knowing" just about everything there is to know (2 Sam 14:20). A reader attentive to context, however, must conclude that her hyperbole finds little basis in reality. David totally misses the danger Amnon poses to Tamar in 2 Sam 13:6–7 as well as the danger Absalom poses to Amnon in 2 Sam 13:26–27. The rape and murder recorded in chapter 13 mirror David's deeply unwise decisions regarding Bathsheba and Uriah in chapter 11, while in episodes to come, the king who supposedly sees everything will catch wind of Absalom's usurpation only in the nick of time. Here are no omniscient "angels of God," whatever the woman from Tekoa might say. Here are foolish men like me.

> Here are no omniscient "angels of God," whatever the woman from Tekoa might say. Here are foolish men like me.

Finally David links Joab's parabolic concoction to his own situation—the banished person (i.e., Absalom) will suffer banishment no longer (2 Sam 14:21; see 14:13–14). And that *feels* like a good and godly response, doesn't it? Joab certainly seems to think so (2 Sam 14:22), but has David really embarked upon the most sagacious path? In reality, no amount of micro-management will contain the fallout from this deeply unwise judgment, for in fetching Absalom home again, David descends only further into life's deepest valley: "Here comes my betrayer!" (Matt 26:46; see 2 Sam 14:23).

☨

When Absalom first arrives in Jerusalem, David declines to communicate with him face to face (2 Sam 14:24). This note implies that even though the problem of Absalom's geographical exclusion has been addressed, the conundrum pertaining to his royal reinstatement persists. The king issues his decree, and of course everyone obeys, but surprise, surprise—David calls fewer shots in the construction of this triple-layer trainwreck than he may think. Any way you slice the cake, the father's sin produces dead children. Here we go again.

Absalom will eventually die while hanging from a tree (2 Sam 18:14), his luxuriant hair tangled in its low-hanging limbs (2 Sam 18:9). Here in chapter 14, his impressive physique would normally signal his fitness for the throne (2 Sam 14:25; see 1 Sam 16:12), but with a special emphasis on Absalom's mane (2 Sam 14:26), the narrator's digression into the prince's appearance at just this point in the text merely foreshadows the story's catastrophic end: "Unless you find a way to see your wounds transformed, you will necessarily transmit them into the next generation." Absalom even names his daughter Tamar (2 Sam 14:27; see 13:22), a rather transparent nod to the fact that virtually everything he does in the book of 2 Samuel rehearses someone else's sin. If David cannot fabricate his House's salvation, still less can his dashing but ill-fated son. Like water spilled upon the ground, so we must die (2 Sam 14:14).

Next Absalom sets fire to Joab's grainfield, an act that generates the invitation to court that David previously refused (2 Sam 14:30–32; see 14:24). If a violent and manipulative Joab beguiles the king into a particular course of unwise action in the chapter's first half, now in the chapter's second half, a violent and manipulative Absalom makes Joab his dutiful servant. Absalom then feigns humble submission, while David—with an ominous "kiss" (see 2 Sam 15:5)—falls for his son's gambit (2 Sam 14:33).

Control, control, control. Three cooks wrestle for one crown mold while an army of rats cleans out the pantry behind them. Where is God in a dysfunctional kitchen such as this?

Absalom presents himself as a generous man-of-the-people (2 Sam 15:1–4), but uses that public persona to "steal" Israel's "heart" (2 Sam 15:6; see 15:13) with a "kiss" (2 Sam 15:5; see 14:33). So begins his newest and greatest lie. In the past, Absalom misled his father so as to create the distance he needed in order to exact retribution on Amnon (2 Sam 13:23–27). Now Absalom leaves David's physical proximity again, to fulfill a vow in Hebron—or so he claims (2 Sam 15:8–9). In the first instance, Absalom cleared away David's heir. In the second, he uses Hebron as a staging ground for the coup (2 Sam 15:10). "Keep your mouth shut and don't take it to heart," indeed (2 Sam 13:20). Better to let David's son pursue his delusions of grandeur unperturbed.

Only when the king's chief counselor, Ahitophel, defects to Absalom's camp does David put two and two together (2 Sam 15:12–13). What are we to make of such cartoonish naïveté? On its surface, the king's ignorance—previously a mark of his reputation for the high moral ground (see 2 Sam 3:26)—does him no favors in the present. How on earth could an "angel of God" (see 2 Sam 14:17, 20) remain so stupid and out of touch? At the same time, however, these details may also orient the reader toward a deeper and more important theological insight that illumines David's character from behind. True, he encourages Absalom to "go in peace" to Hebron (2 Sam 15:9), which, from the perspective of *Realpolitik*, constitutes perhaps the biggest blunder he ever makes. But his salvation also begins (necessarily, as all twelve-steppers know) with submission and release. In the face of Absalom's renewed effort to wield a "sword" against his extended family, David commits himself to an exilic path (2 Sam 15:14). For the first time since chapter 12, the foolish dancer lets go.

Leaving behind ten concubines to keep the house (a crucial plot point that resurfaces in chapter 16), David and his followers depart Jerusalem like deported slaves (2 Sam 15:16–17). This surprising evacuation from the urban center that bears the king's name brings loyalists and non-loyalists out of the woodwork, while David's conversations with these individuals provide the text's implied author with an occasion to underscore the iconographic significance of his flight. At a purely practical level, the first three of these interviews focus on whether the loyalist in view should stay behind in Jerusalem or join David's band of refugees. Ittai the Gittite glues himself to the king's side (2 Sam 15:19–22) while Zadok and Abiathar, the Ark's priestly caretakers, are sent back to work as informers from the inside out (2 Sam 15:24–29, 35–36). Hushai the Arkite, too, returns to Jerusalem with orders to "frustrate" (2 Sam 15:34) Absalom's plans from within (2 Sam 15:32–37). As these minor characters head off in their respective directions, the text's center of gravity remains fixed on the catastrophic danger that threatens to sweep David from the pages of Israelite memory, while its word choice matters here like nowhere else. The narrator repeatedly portrays David as "crossing over" or "passing through" (2 Sam 15:23–24; see 15:28, 15:33, 16:1) into exile while the Promised Land breaks down in tears all around (2 Sam 15:23; see 15:30). Barefoot and weeping, the Lord's Anointed travels the road before him as the historical and literary personification of his people's sins (2 Sam 15:30).

Idou ho anthrōpos. Hinneh ha'ish.

> Barefoot and weeping, the Lord's Anointed travels the road before him as the historical and literary personification of his people's sins.

Does Punishment spoil the House? Or does it sweep the floor? An incalculable paradox lies hidden in 2 Samuel's heart of hearts, articulated perhaps most succinctly in Nathan's mysterious claim that, "the Lord has 'crossed out' your sin; you will not die" (2 Sam 12:13). In this way, David's triumphal entry transforms into a Via Dolorosa, a tear-stained boulevard leading from the Garden of Gethsemane up to the Olive Mount. It's all about God's strange math (see 2 Sam 14:14).

☩

My wife and I were engaged in the winter of 2018. We were both thirty-nine years old at the time, and for me, the early summer wedding for which we began to prepare would be my second. If kids in their early twenties race to the altar for reasons of sex and romance, damaged souls in their late thirties do so from the fear of dying alone. Is this love?, we had asked each other over and over again throughout the previous fall. Does it heal wounds? Do we really want to spend the rest of our lives together, or are we simply desperate for a drug potent enough to take away the pain?

Weddings of the former type function like rites of passage. As if receiving a first driver's license or walking in a college graduation, the couple transitions from one phase of young adulthood into a future drunk on adventure and hope. Images of distinct childhoods, lived hundreds of miles apart but set to anthems appropriate to the decade, gradually converge on the experiences and activities through which the lovers realized their common bond. Emotions run on overdrive; endorphins surge. Forty-dollar unity candles (when did that gimmick begin?) and readings from 1 Corinthians 13 (context reliably omitted) take center stage in what remains—lest the signatories forget—a legal contract.

When brides and grooms in their late thirties marry one another, however, they have often filed divorce papers at some point in the relatively recent past, whether they wanted to or not. They show up sober and broken, and it shows. What bright-eyed and bushy-tailed twenty-year-old features "By Way of Sorrow" by Julie Miller as the ceremony's musical interlude? What unscathed child opts for a rare hymn like "Pensive, Doubting, Fearful Heart," based on the anguish and relief of Isaiah 54? When I married for the first time, I simply did not yet have "cause to grieve," that I should want to be reminded of "what the God of love can do."[35] Thus the unfurled banners and major marches of wedding number one were replaced, at wedding number two, by minor chords and muted trumpets. A lingering sadness—palpable throughout the ceremony that my wife and I composed ourselves—salted the cake before it was even cut.

Is this love?, I asked her with my eyes while leaning forward for the kiss. Will it heal our wounds?, she replied as we circled each other at the dance. There was a time in my life when I would have judged the perceived "impurity" of a second wedding as a sign of its inferiority. Now that I have passed through one of these complicated celebrations for myself, I confess that I must scrap my naïveté, for the way of love has proven less straightforward than I had imagined in my youth. "Purity" doesn't even make the list (see 1 Cor 13:4–6), an observation more obvious in one's forties, perhaps, than in one's twenties. Love is dirty; love is difficult. Love mourns and laments. Love is a trainwreck and a grade-A mess. Love is a magnificent defeat. Love is a total waste of time. "The one I kiss is the man; arrest him" (Matt 26:48), and in response, "Jesus Christ laid down his life for us" (1 John 3:16). Yes, yes, yes.

Betrayed by a Kiss

As David lets go of his former glory, he is shadowed by a man named Shimei, a member of Saul's dynastic dead end and therefore a salient reminder of the destination to which exile ungoverned by Promise eventually leads. Shimei "curses" (see 2 Sam 6:22) David to his face while "hurling stones" at him (2 Sam 16:5–6; see 16:13). For this disenfranchised son of Saul, David remains an unnuanced tyrant and thief, a "man of blood" who now undergoes the Punishment marked out for him by his previous crimes (2 Sam 16:7–8).

Joab's brother, Abishai, immediately perceives and adjudicates the offense. Such disrespect, he argues, warrants a response vigorous enough to deter any further assaults against the king: "Let me cross over," he says to David, "so that I can remove his head" (2 Sam 16:9). Tit for tat, eye for eye, wound for wound (see 2 Sam 3:27). In the same way that both Saul and Ishbosheth suffer a beheading (1 Sam 31:9; 2 Sam 4:7), a "dead dog" like Shimei should suffer, too (2 Sam 16:9; see 3:8, 9:8). Politically speaking, now is no time for mercy.

If the reader is paying close attention, however, Abishai's legal excitement betrays his theological confusion, for 2 Samuel's strangely intertwined acts of "crossing out" sin and "crossing over" into exile do not present David with an opportunity to shore up his dynastic achievements by tightening the screws on his political enemies. Rather, they guide him onto a twelve-step staircase that descends into the valley of submission and release. For all his apparent "ignorance" in 2 Samuel 13–15, here David wisely rejects his Mighty-Man's violent huffing and puffing. After all, he reasons, Shimei may be an integral part of God's plan; his insults may simply comprise an unavoidable hairpin turn on the mountain trail below his bare, blistered feet (2 Sam 16:10). So go on, says the once-majestic king, now running for his life (2 Sam 16:11): curse me with curses, stone me with stones, and dust me with dust (see 2 Sam 16:13). Perhaps God will get involved in my dysfunction. Perhaps God will transform my mess (2 Sam 16:12). Either way, "I will become even more cursed than this, and I will become abased in my own eyes" (2 Sam 6:22). David performs another Boogie-Woogie. You can strip him down and you can hurl rocks at his head, but you cannot strip naked nakedness itself.

English-language translations of 2 Sam 16:6 usually rely on two words to express Shimei's act of "throwing rocks" or "hurling stones" at David, but Hebrew communicates the same idea with a more compact, three-letter root: *sql*. As literary providence would have it, the pronunciation of this term in its various conjugations can sound almost identical to forms of another three-letter root, *skl*, which has to do with being "foolish." Reminded of his chief counselor's defection in 2 Sam 15:31 (see 2 Sam 15:12), David asks God to "make foolish" Ahitophel's wise counsel before Absalom. Stone the stones; curse the curse; turn the Punishment inside out.

> David asks God to "make foolish" Ahitophel's wise counsel before Absalom. Stone the stones; curse the curse; turn the Punishment inside out.

It is a truism of 2 Samuel research to say that commentators typically locate the answer to this prayer in the work of Hushai the Arkite, David's friend and confidante who returns to Jerusalem (2 Sam 15:37) under explicit orders to "frustrate" Ahitophel's good advice (2 Sam 15:34; see 17:14). For indeed, Hushai does exactly what David commands: he feigns allegiance to Absalom (2 Sam 16:16–19; see 15:34) and then diverts the usurping prince from putting into motion Ahitophel's superior plan of attack (2 Sam 17:1–14). The reader may notice, however, that Ahitophel's counsel actually consists of *two* major elements, not one, and it is only the second (having to do with Absalom's military strategy; 2 Sam 17:1–4) that Hushai addresses and deconstructs (2 Sam 17:7–13). While this conversation transpires, the first element of Ahitophel's counsel lingers about the story like the smell of a musty basement. "What should I do now?" Absalom asks his chief wise man (2 Sam 16:20). "Have sex with your father's concubines," Ahitophel replies (2 Sam 16:21; see 2 Sam 15:16). "Unless you find a way to see your wounds transformed...."

The aspiring king pursues this politically advantageous but morally bankrupt course of action straightaway, and once again, the implied author's word choice plays an outsized role in the text's theological significance. The tenfold rape in Tamar's honor (see 2 Sam 13:20; 20:3) takes place in public—"on the roof" (see 2 Sam 11:2) and before "the eyes of all Israel" (2 Sam 16:22). In other words, the highly specific effect of the self-annihilating sword that Nathan predicted in 2 Samuel 12 has finally come to pass: "I will raise up against you trouble from within your own House, and I will take your wives before your eyes and I will give them to your neighbor, who will lie with your wives before the eyes of the sun. For you acted in secret, but I will do this thing in front of all Israel, in broad daylight" (2 Sam 12:11–12). Remember that the counsel of Ahitophel was, in those days, tantamount to the word of God (2 Sam 16:23). And that counsel equates to Punishment all the way down.

Thus, to paraphrase, David asks God to "make foolish" Nathan's divine word (2 Sam 15:31)! Stone the stones; curse the curse; turn sin's tragic repercussions inside out. Make the sword a hidden Pathway into hope: "For the foolishness of God is wiser than human wisdom, and the weakness of God is stronger than human strength" (1 Cor 1:25).

The more I reflect upon my institutionally sanctioned awesomeness, the saltier I become. I am disappointed in my Self. I am betrayed by *The Kiss*. And so I fling my withered corpse onto the words of Isaiah 54:

> *Though afflicted, tempest-tossed,*
> *Comfortless awhile thou art,*
> *Do not think thou canst be lost,*
> *Thou art graven on my heart;*
> *All thy wastes I will repair;*
> *Thou shalt be rebuilt anew;*
> *And in thee it shall appear*
> *What the God of love can do.*[36]

Astonishingly, the pseudo-wisdom of the woman from Tekoa proves prophetically accurate, though perhaps not in the manner that Joab or David anticipated at the time. God really does devise ways so that a banished person may not remained estranged from him (2 Sam 14:14). God recalculates our diseased culture's worst advice from the inside out. The Law breaks my heart, but then the Lawmaker sutures the incision and holds me tight while I cry, cry, cry away the pain.

As we repeated our vows at the altar and made our public promises, her desert unfurled into flower. My wasteland erupted with color (Isa 35:1–10). Every day since then we have learned a little bit more about what it means to lay down our lives for one another (1 John 3:16). This is our love song—the Song of Solomon. And love heals wounds.

7

Hanging from a Tree

(2 Samuel 17–20)

*I can't think for you, you'll have to decide
Whether Judas Iscariot had God on his side.*

Bob Dylan, "With God on Our Side"

We learn in 2 Sam 15:12 that Ahitophel the free agent has signed with a new team. His treason stems from the fact that Absalom has already hatched a coup (2 Sam 15:1–6), but of course, the prince's factionalism also does not pop out of thin air. It derives (at least in part) from David's inadequate solution to Absalom's banishment as described in 2 Samuel 14. Meanwhile, Absalom fled into exile (2 Sam 13:37–38) in the first place only because he murdered Amnon (2 Sam 13:28–29), a crime directly inspired by Amnon's prior sexual assault against Absalom's sister, Tamar (2 Sam 13:22, 32). Finally, the reader should have no trouble in remembering that this trio of doomed siblings remains the product of one man with a passion for himself. Fresh propaganda will be written and patriotism will surge anew, old maps will be dusted off and new trenches will be dug, but any way you slice the cake, war is suicide. Lions and zebras: this is who we are.

In what direction, then, does God lean when the jungle king's pride rips apart his "pride"? For which sports franchise does God root? Which network news does God prefer? The reader may detect an answer to this question in the fact that divine providence appears to stack the deck for David when he needs it most: "Make foolish the counsel of Ahitophel, O Lord!" (2 Sam 15:31). Timely words, for without question, Ahitophel's gameplan would deliver the league trophy to Absalom in a blowout (2 Sam 17:1–4) were it not for David's inside man. Hushai the Arkite suggests to Absalom that despite Ahitophel's well-deserved reputation for interpreting the signs of the times, in this case his proposal contains a fatal flaw (2 Sam 17:7). David isn't weak and running scared, says Hushai—he's a mother bear robbed of his cubs (2 Sam 17:8). He's an experienced outlaw with a thousand underground tunnels in which to hide (2 Sam 17:9). He's a battlefield champion who has slain his giants (2 Sam 17:10). Better, therefore, to pursue victory by means of overwhelming force than by speed (2 Sam 17:11–13). The ruse works. Absalom and his court adjust their plans (2 Sam 17:14), giving David a chance to regroup. Here the narrator could not be more theologically explicit, for the story's turning point (and the beginning of the end for David's son) comes about only because of God's abiding superintendence over the plot: "The Lord had determined to frustrate Ahitophel's good counsel in order to bring Absalom to ruin" (2 Sam 17:14). Moreover, when Hushai tells Zadok and Abiathar what happened at court (2 Sam 17:15–16), fortune continues to swing in David's direction. A woman in Bahurim hides the priests' sons in a well so that the information gets through (2 Sam 17:17–21; see Josh 2:4–7). All such evidence leads to the same conclusion: God remains David's biggest fan, right?

I am not so sure. Yes, God brings about ruin for one biblical character while orchestrating military success for his rival, but does that truth equate to a straightforward game of partisan politics? When David hears (at least a portion of) what transpired during Absalom's conferences with Ahitophel and Hushai, he responds to the messengers' urgent advice to "cross over" the Jordan River as quickly as possible (2 Sam 17:21) by "crossing over" the Jordan River as quickly as possible (2 Sam 17:22). It's curious that God's stacked deck generates not immediate triumph for David but a darker and a more thorough exile. At the same time, the repetitive language of "crossing out" and "crossing over" that characterizes David's Punishment infuses the whole experience with an undeniable echo of Promise: "The Lord has 'crossed out' your sin; you will not die" (2 Sam 12:13; see 7:14–15). The paradoxical conflation of these contradictory ideas alerts the reader to the book's complex theology. God does not occupy a clear-cut "side" in this contest. Instead, the story of David and Absalom *in toto* offers us a stained-glass window into the whole, human problem, and as such, under no possible circumstances can either party win the ensuing war, for the battle that each man prepares to fight is a battle waged against his own flesh and blood. Winning is not the point. Winning is *never* the point. The book of 2 Samuel does not portray a deity who swears reluctant fealty to David's religio-political ambitions; it narrates God's free choice to construct an edifice of God's own, mysterious design (see Ps 127:1). David, Bathsheba, Uriah, Joab, Amnon, Tamar, Absalom, and Solomon merely comprise the rotten and reclaimed timbers with which the builder works. No victors allowed.

> Under no possible circumstances can either party win the ensuing war, for the battle that each man prepares to fight is a battle waged against his own flesh and blood.

☦

As 2 Samuel's plot accelerates toward Absalom's doom, a brief but arresting sidebar appears in 2 Sam 17:23. Sagacious Ahitophel saddles his donkey, puts his house in order, and hangs himself on the nearest tree. Suicides are rare in Christian Scripture (e.g., see Judg 9:54; 1 Sam 31:4), but one in particular seems a close cousin to the text at hand. Near the end of Matthew's Gospel, another crafty politician likewise opts for the rope and stool (Matt 27:3–5). Both men betray their Davidic king; both men take their lives as a result.

From one angle, the choice to sell Jesus to the authorities for thirty pieces of silver (Matt 26:14–16; see Mark 14:10–11) defies imagination. Given that Judas Iscariot lived and worked with Jesus for some time prior to his betrayal, enjoying all the benefits of membership in Jesus's inner circle, his rationale can be difficult for present-day disciples to comprehend. From another angle, however, Judas's behavior still manages to read like an embarrassingly familiar vice, for every one of us makes moral exceptions from time to time—often in the name of financial security. How, therefore, does one account for such an outrageous yet commonplace crime? How do we make sense of the fact that one of Jesus's closest friends wound up shoving a knife through his abdomen? The Gospel of John deals with this question by emphasizing Judas's love of money at a prior point in the narrative, thereby providing an explanation for his later treachery (John 12:4–6), while also identifying Judas as a person under satanic influence (John 6:70; 13:2, 27).

Hanging from a Tree

Luke's Gospel supports the latter claim (Luke 22:3), but does not dwell on the subject in the same way that John does. Instead, the book of Acts goes on to highlight the corporeal consequences of Judas's actions by reporting that his bloated corpse eventually burst open in what must have been an especially putrid scene (Acts 1:18). Thus, if interpreted in sum, the New Testament portrays the human habit of stabbing Christ in the back as illogical, unprofitable, demonic, self-destructive, and gross.

Giovanni Canavesio, *The Suicide of Judas* (1491)[37]

By contrast, the characteristically reticent Old Testament does not explore Ahitophel's reasons for supporting Absalom instead of David. Readers sometimes hypothesize that he harbored a vendetta,[38] since Ahitophel was apparently Bathsheba's grandfather (see 2 Sam 11:3; 23:34), but in reality, the text does not clarify or even mention motive. Ahitophel neither accepts money in exchange for his treachery nor does he act under the influence of an evil spirit. His suicide likewise occurs without fanfare or embellishment. Nevertheless, the fundamental mistake that both Ahitophel and Judas make—of which the New Testament betrayer's infamous kiss is only a symptom—remains identical. Both men pick a team in a contest that the God of love intends to subvert. The same criticism applies also to the disciple (i.e., Simon Peter) who cuts off Malchus's ear (Matt 26:51; John 18:10). In each of these cases, the individual makes an exception for violence in order to achieve a purported good of his own, imaginative design, presuming that the dog-eat-dog world in which we live conforms, without alternative, to a law of zero sums. Darwinian conquistadors and Galápagos tortoises all the way down—this is who we are. But Jesus refuses to play their nihilistic game. The Lover does not bite. "Put your sword back in its place . . . for all who draw the sword will die by the sword" (Matt 26:52; see 2 Sam 12:10). Narrative irony does the rest. What began as a smart man's economic advantage suddenly morphs into a stomach-turning act of self-destruction, while by contrast, what must have looked like sheer suicide to Jesus's other disciples (he's not even going to resist?) births a community characterized by self-giving love: "Jesus Christ laid down his life for us" (1 John 3:16). The Son of David dives headfirst into his ancestor's Punishment and there, at the very bottom of all things, barefoot and weeping in the Garden of human misery, transforms the world's wars from the inside out.

☩

When Catholic artist James Tissot painted Absalom's death, he made an intriguing modification to his Old Testament source. According to the text, Joab rebukes the soldier who first finds Absalom alive and kicking in the tree, and then (taking the matter into his own hands) drives three rods through Absalom's heart (2 Sam 18:14). This act of violence could hardly have eluded Tissot, for the whole drama builds up to and then climaxes in the prince's shockingly brutal death. Preceding verses describe how Absalom, upon recognizing the failure of his military effort against David (2 Sam 18:7), tries to escape on a mule. The mule rides through a woody thicket that catches in Absalom's beautiful hair (see 2 Sam 14:26) and then lifts him from his saddle as the animal "crosses over" underneath, leaving him to dangle helplessly "between heaven and earth" (2 Sam 18:9). In other words, Absalom becomes a low-hanging apple that Joab—regardless of David's instructions to "deal gently" in 2 Sam 18:5—eagerly plucks. Tissot faithfully reproduces several of these details, such as Absalom's tangled locks, his suspension from a tree, and his death by impaling. Yet the picture certainly does not show three stakes protruding from the dead man's chest. Pierced by six arrows instead, 2 Samuel's archetypal betrayer becomes a mirror of Sebastian, the third-century saint and martyr under Diocletian. David's Judas . . . wears a halo!

James Tissot, *La mort d'Absalon* (1904)[39]

Why should the reader shed even one drop for Absalom, of all people? His character resembles *nothing* of Christ. He is a murderer, thief, liar, traitor, and rapist. He is the architect of unspeakable suffering; he designs and prosecutes yet another of humanity's suicidal wars. It's not like the Old Testament paints him as a tragically misunderstood artist desperate for his father's approval. No, Absalom dies like Achan dies, and deservedly so. Buried under a pile of stones (2 Sam 18:17; see Josh 7:25–26), he becomes an enduring monument to humanity's self-conceit (2 Sam 18:18). Never did a Bible character less deserve a little mercy now.

When faced with the prospect of destroying his own son, however, the man after God's own heart orders compassion (2 Sam 18:5). We know nothing about David's hopes and anxieties at this point in the text, for as usual, Old Testament narrative does not pursue such rabbit trails. But we do not need to know what sort of private anguish David "really felt" in order to appreciate what he says and does. The exilic king gestures toward an alternative, a third way that cuts between the trenches rapidly deepening on either side of a Punishment he cannot avoid. "Deal gently," he says (2 Sam 18:5); tread lightly. Remember that winning is not the point.

Again, any text-responsible summary of Absalom's life must conclude that he looks nothing like Christ with regard to ambition and behavior. Yet through Christ's undeserving death, God becomes the spitting image of David's mangled son. His hair caught in thorny branches, and while hanging from a tree, Jesus watches his political future go up in smoke. Iron nails penetrate his body from head to toe. The lions unzip his belly (John 19:34); Joab's merciless knife reaches to the heart. "God made him who had no sin to be sin for us" (2 Cor 5:21)—so the King of kings becomes human excrement, an utter waste of breath.

☩

Absalom's failed usurpation requires some additional mopping up in 2 Samuel 19, but the acute danger that it poses to David throughout 2 Samuel 15–17 begins to relax now that the usurper lies dead under a small mountain of rocks. That said, the king's physical and intellectual distance from the action gives 2 Samuel's implied author an opportunity to build fresh tension on a new front, culminating in a second climax distinct from the first. The battle may be "won," but how will David react to the loss of yet another son (see 2 Sam 12:19–20; 13:31, 36)?

News in the ancient world was delivered in person rather than by wires and waves, and that takes time. Still, the text could easily summarize this dimension of the plot in a verse, a half verse, or even less: somebody or other relays the battle's outcome to David. Instead, it lingers (even dawdles) on the context that frames David's latest encounter with Nathan's sword. The chapter portrays two couriers under Joab's command rather than only one—loyal Ahimaaz (see 2 Sam 17:17-21) and an unnamed Cushite about whom the reader has no other information. At Joab's direction, the Cushite leaves the battlefield first (2 Sam 18:21) while Ahimaaz leaves second (2 Sam 18:23), even though the latter character eventually outruns the former (2 Sam 18:27). Either way, both heralds carry the same information. Both know exactly what has transpired under Joab's command. Both know that Absalom has become a corpse.

While these puzzle pieces fall into place, the reader enjoys a momentary reprieve from the action-packed first half of 2 Samuel 18—a chance to catch his or her breath. Simultaneously, the narrative lull invites fresh consideration of what must soon take place. Is the news carried by Ahimaaz and the Cushite good or bad? And does that question even make sense in a prophetic no man's land where winning is not the point?

As Ahimaaz approaches, David assumes that his servant's fine character indicates a good report (2 Sam 18:27). And upon arrival, "Peace!" leaps from Ahimaaz's mouth, which certainly sounds like a positive result—peace, peace, where there was no peace before (2 Sam 18:28). But is the "peace" you have won, asks David, a zero-sum sort of peace (2 Sam 18:29)? Did it require my son's annihilation? In response, Ahimaaz (now markedly less enthusiastic about delivering his message; see 2 Sam 18:22-23) appears to waffle, which forces David to wait a little longer before finding out the truth (2 Sam 18:29-30). So the water rises even higher, licking the levy's lips in the tense minutes before a catastrophic breach.

> Is the news carried by Ahimaaz and the Cushite good or bad? And does that question even make sense in a prophetic no man's land where winning is not the point?

Next the Cushite arrives, and again David pursues an answer to his fundamental question: not "Who won?," but "What kind of a win did we achieve?" Peace, peace, returns the Cushite—but there is no peace. "May the enemies of my lord the king," he says, "become like [Absalom]" (2 Sam

18:32). In the topsy-turvy world of David's exilic "cross over," good news is bad news and bad news is good (see 2 Sam 19:3). No victors allowed.

☩

The news instantly washes David off his precipice, down into an ocean of grief. No degree of familiarity with Old Testament narration and dialogue sufficiently prepares the reader of 2 Samuel for the reverberations of lament found in chapter 18, verse 33,[40] for within the biblical canon, only Jeremiah's ragged lyricism seems to compare. Repetitive and raw, it fills up the reader's senses like a tsunami lifting away the wreckage of the life you've lost. "My son, Absalom—my son, my son! Absalom, Absalom—my son, my son!" (2 Sam 18:33; see 19:4).

The "upper room" (2 Sam 18:33) is an iconic location in Scripture, a place where a king may easily succumb to fatal injury (see 2 Kgs 1:2, 17), such as evisceration by means of a double-edged sword (see Judg 3:20–21). The venue may stage a supreme act of humility as well (see John 13:2–5), but only if it generates a corresponding stab in the back (see John 13:21–27). Over and over again, upper rooms contain sickbeds and suffering, destruction and death. And precisely for that reason, they also, on special occasions, become temples to the Old Testament's God of resurrection (see 1 Kgs 17:19–21; 2 Kgs 4:34–35). I have climbed to the top of St. Paul's, whose Romanesque architecture certainly steals away one's breath. But the church's best theology is not found in its lofty arches. Mark you the dusty, checkered floor?

No sooner has mourning for Absalom commenced than Joab reminds David that he has not yet escaped his enemy's noose. Everything depends now on his willingness to affirm that the battle has produced a positive result (2 Sam 19:5–7). According to Joab, public success and private tears do not mix, and from the perspective of *Realpolitik*, he is right. God's inverted "crossroad" does not apply. Victors do not mourn their enemies, scholars do not fail, and winners do not confess. C'mon, David—buck up and be awesome!

St. Paul's Cathedral Nave, London[41]

The remainder of 2 Samuel 19 describes the political minefield that David must navigate in order to regain his throne in Jerusalem. What to do with the large number of people who participated in Absalom's rebellion but who, unlike the prince, remain alive and well? Perhaps signaling his interest in conciliation, David promises to replace Joab with Amasa, Absalom's army captain (2 Sam 19:13; see 17:25), as a part of the deal. Down to the Jordan River "crossing" he therefore goes (2 Sam 19:15), where exile runs in reverse. The people's stolen "heart" reverts to its first love (2 Sam 19:14; see 15:6)—at least for now.

At this point in the text, David undergoes a series of encounters with a variety of familiar individuals, in a kind of rehearsal of the cameos that make up 2 Samuel 15–17. When running for his life, his conversations with these minor characters were marked by concrete expressions of either loyalty (e.g., Ittai, Zadok and Abiathar, Hushai, Ziba, and Barzillai) or extreme disloyalty (e.g., Mephibosheth [by uncorroborated hearsay] and Shimei). In the aftermath of Absalom's death, however, this crisp distinction between friends and enemies evaporates, leaving the king awash in political shades of gray. Shimei repents dramatically of what he said to David in chapter 16—but does he really mean it (2 Sam 19:16–23)? Then disheveled Mephibosheth appears, claiming that Ziba has slandered him—but why can't David properly adjudicate between the two men's mutually exclusive claims (2 Sam 19:24–30)? Trusty Barzillai, who gave David food, supplies, and rest when he needed it most (2 Sam 17:27–29), now seems reluctant to get any further involved (2 Sam 19:31–40). In all these cases, shouldn't the inverse obtain instead? Neither do David's restored fortunes produce a satisfying, public feast as the reader might expect (see 2 Sam 6:19). Instead, the king hardly sets one foot on the Jordan's western bank before Israel's factionalism launches the people of God into yet another, suicidal war (2 Sam 19:41—20:2; see 2 Sam 20:4–22). Shouldn't *Punishment* generate the murky bog, while David's triumphant return opens onto a bright and bubbly future? Strange that God's reinvigorated Promise should follow so ambiguous and incomplete a path. Where's the happy ending?

> Strange that God's reinvigorated Promise should follow so ambiguous and incomplete a path. Where's the happy ending?

As ever, the implied author's narrative style and peculiar choice of words point the reader toward a theological horizon beyond his or her probable disappointment with the facts on the ground. If the conversations in which David participates throughout 2 Sam 19:15–43 offer no clear escape from the political swamp, they nevertheless suggest shadows of a solution to the reader, as if glimpsed through a glass darkly (see 1 Cor 13:12). Shimei, for example, begs David not to "calculate" the grave offense that he committed in 2 Sam 16:7–8 (2 Sam 19:19; see 14:14). True to form, Abishai reasserts his original point, that Shimei's crime requires a mathematical response, applied by means of a Law-enforcing sword (2 Sam 19:21; see 16:9). But David has had enough of the Zeruiah family's harsh arithmetic (2 Sam 19:22–23). Climbing the steep road up to Jerusalem (see 2 Sam 15:30), the king undergoes another figurative descent, twelve steps down into the basement of his royal acumen. The return from exile proves no different, really, from the exile itself. Both the Punishment and the Promise—David's self-annihilating sword and his durable House—remain mysteriously saturated with the language of the "cross" (2 Sam 19:15, 18, 31, 33, 36–41). It's the "F"s that set us Free.

Everywhere the reader looks in the carefully constructed and utterly depressing episode that follows 2 Samuel 19, he or she will find images of human waste. A "worthless" man (see 2 Sam 16:7) named Sheba son of Bikri incites the northern tribes to break away from their southern neighbors (2 Sam 20:1–2). One war breeds another.

The new conflict presents an occasion for David to make good on his promise to Amasa (see 2 Sam 19:13), so the king begins his next campaign by commanding the former rebel to muster Judah's army (2 Sam 20:4–5). Sheba's forces seem to require everything David can throw at them, however, so he sends Joab and Abishai into battle as well (2 Sam 20:6–7). With all three men out the door, and with David once again cloistered from the action, a day marked by manly exploits does not go unseized. Joab feigns "peace" and goodwill toward Amasa, but betrays him with a kiss (2 Sam 20:9; see 14:33; 15:5). *Carpe homo*. He then shoves a knife through Amasa's abdomen (2 Sam 20:10; see 2:23; 3:27; 4:6), spilling his entrails on the ground (see Acts 1:18). As Joab's army rubbernecks a murder scene for the second time in this book (2 Sam 20:11; see 2:23), the text does not shy away from the stomach-turning sight they behold. Neither should the reader. Dying quickly, Amasa writhes in his blood like an eviscerated zebra. And as if this grotesque image were not enough, Joab soon finds himself besieging a city full of his own countrymen (2 Sam 20:15; cf. 11:1). Another "wise woman" appears (2 Sam 20:16; see 14:2), but of course the reader knows enough by now to require a little proof of said wisdom before taking the adjective at face value. The woman's savvy language and political skill convince Joab to suspend his all-out assault on her hometown, thus saving it from destruction (2 Sam 20:16–22)—a "smart" move indeed, except that the salvation upon which Joab and the woman agree requires the severed head of yet another human soul, heaved like an egg over the city wall with a snap, crackle, and pop (2 Sam 20:21–22). The

> The text's newest scoundrel may become a headless corpse by chapter's end, but for every dead Sheba, ten million more await the draft.

typology of sin should be obvious: Abner begets Joab, Joab begets Amasa, Ishbosheth begets Sheba, Tekoa begets Abel Beth Maakah. David fathers "trustworthy" Amnon, and Amnon "fathers" Ab-*shalom*. What a mess! The text's newest scoundrel may become a headless corpse by chapter's end, but for every dead Sheba, ten million more await the draft. Every war is a civil dead end; every war is suicide. Thus we wrap up the present saga exactly where we began, with a poignant reflection on David's political and dynastic achievements (2 Sam 20:23–26): no victors allowed.

Curious that the biblical narrator—when moving from the argument that David encounters at the Jordan River to that argument's rapid devolution into armed conflict—should bother to remember the ten rape survivors of 2 Sam 16:22 and their perpetual widowhood (2 Sam 20:3; see 13:20). The note cannot help but recall Ahitophel's sage advice ("Have sex with your father's concubines"; 2 Sam 16:21), which David prayed that God would "make foolish" (2 Sam 15:31). Is the verse a clunky non sequitur, or a vital clue?

The story of David as told in the book of 2 Samuel is the story of a tearful flood, a broken dam gushing human failure onto an Israelite wheatfield. Viewed from one angle, such floods accomplish very little. Humanity ruins the earth (Gen 6:5), so God ruins humanity (Gen 6:7–8), but in the end, humanity remains a ruined mess (Gen 9:20–27). What's the point of a deluge if the problem simply reasserts itself when the waters recede? Did God overlook the fact that "two of every kind" (Gen 6:19) would necessarily include the Snakes? Viewed from another angle, however, floods become vehicles for hope. Through ultimate catastrophe, God offers creation a first impression of the enduring love by which it will be saved—nothing short of broken light (Gen 9:13; see Isa 54:9; John 8:12).

What David needs is what the whole world needs—not "victory," but baptism and Sabbath rest. We need a year of Jubilee, a moment of reprieve—time and space enough to weep for the tragedy of our condition. We need a third way. We need death and resurrection. As it stands, charges will continue to be filed and cases will continue to be decided, lands will be allocated and favors granted, new enemies will arise and new insurrections will be quelled. The political machine chugs on. All the while, David's grief-stricken words ricochet from one tragic page of this prophetic book to the next: "My son, Absalom! Absalom, my son, my son! Would that I had died instead of you!" (2 Sam 18:33).

8

Worship and Waste

(2 Samuel 21–24)

Abundant waters cannot extinguish love,
and rivers cannot overwhelm it.
If one were to give all the wealth of one's house in exchange for love,
it would be utterly scorned.

SONG OF SOLOMON 8:7

"Consider how the wild flowers grow. They do not labor or spin. Yet I tell you, not even Solomon in all his splendor was dressed like one of these. If that is how God clothes the grass of the field, which is here today, and tomorrow is thrown into the fire, how much more will he clothe you—you of little faith!"

LUKE 12:27–28

DEAD POETS SOCIETY was nominated for several Academy Awards in 1990, including best picture and best screenplay. The film tracks a group of wealthy, white, male teenagers enrolled at an elite boarding school in Vermont, and shortly after the new term begins, Walt Whitman's *Song of*

Myself transforms their world from the inside out. Contemporary children of the culture that Whitman helped to define (i.e., anyone who listens to pop) will connect intuitively with the poem's rollicking free verse, its pronounced use of the first and second persons, and its quasi-religious Romanticism. What image could be more self-justifying and self-possessed than a narratorial "spotted hawk"—"not a bit tamed" and "untranslatable"—sounding its "barbaric yawp over the roofs of the world"?[42] Perhaps only Katy Perry's predictable idea that she possesses "the eye of a tiger" and that "you're gonna hear me roar."[43] These assertions (as well as all those in between) go down like shots of perfectly distilled, 200 proof, Kentucky humanism. I admit that once upon a time I became deeply enamored with Robert Sean Leonard's passion and supposed bravery, but the nineties are ancient history, and I am no longer a sixteen-year-old boy. Now I am a man—more specifically, I am a post-surgery Achilles patient with fillings in his teeth, grinding away at the grave, and "My Way" just hasn't delivered what Hollywood always promised it would. As the Canadian birders with whom I now rub shoulders enjoy pointing out, the bald eagle remains an unrepentant kleptoparasite. Whit Stillman was right: "What if 'thine own self' is not so good? What if it's pretty bad?"[44]

On its surface, Israel's Song of Solomon may suggest a few points of comparison with America's archetypal *Song of Myself*. Tradition associates the book with a single, male author who shifts back and forth between the first and second persons. Moreover, like no other Scripture, the text revels in passionate, thinly veiled celebrations of the human body. But there the similarities end, for Old Testament literature in general (written by whole communities rather than by charismatic individuals) expresses a premodern anthropology very different from Whitman's. The book features not a quintessential "I," but two "I"s engaged in a deeply intimate conversation wherein each also serves as the other's "you." Conscious of his sizzling desire, the lover gathers up his words and spreads them out for his beloved like a feast. Acutely aware of her frustration, the beloved finds temporary relief by directing toward her lover expressions of hunger and thirst even greater than those he lavishes on her. Meanwhile, the reader becomes a witness to their steamy love affair, but not as a voyeur peeping in on a male author's autoeroticism. Instead, he or she joins an ecclesial chorus that blesses (and is blessed by) every sun-soaked inch of the couple's sexual anticipation. Solomon's Song, in other words, is all about the people of God, not the autonomous lone wolf. It's a poem

Worship and Waste

about love, and the essence of love is gift (see 1 John 3:16). In this way, the book becomes a Sabbath rest for its reader—a year of Jubilee. It's a walled Garden of lost language, replanted and restored. It's theological ecstasy, unlimited reward, and worship without reduction. It's a rare reprieve from a world hellbent on suicide. Everything else—no matter how romantic the author's ideas may seem—is just another form of war.

The literary contrast described above may help to frame a question at the heart of 2 Samuel's challenging, four-chapter conclusion. When all is said and done, what kind of a song does David sing in chapter 22? The first and most obvious conclusion that one could reach in response to this inquiry identifies the text as a psalm—a worship poem almost identical, in fact, to Psalm 18. This observation may suggest that the implied author of 2 Samuel intends to portray David's reverence and humility before God, since the very same verses function in a different location as the reader's prayer book. When 2 Samuel 22 appears in that other context, the reader naturally adopts its language for him or herself, offering the verses back to God while reflecting on David's story. Lodged within the Former Prophets, however, the same text does not necessarily perform in the same way. Here the protagonist on the page prays Psalm 18, not the reader. His words certainly give us something to pray *about*, but that fact does not automatically mean that we should follow a hermeneutical principle of "monkey see, monkey do," which proves a very bad idea on numerous other occasions. The book of Jonah, for example, puts a psalm of repentance and thanksgiving into its main character's mouth, but the Bible's all-time worst (yet ironically successful) preacher does not then transform into a model pastor for his Assyrian enemies. Likewise, we cannot rule out the possibility, *a priori*, that David's prayer functions as a deconstructive exposé of his deluded ambition rather than as a blueprint for the reader's piety.[45] If only we could reconstruct the inner workings of David's mind, says the modern psycho-exegete, then the interpretive fog would lift.

So what does David "really think" when he sings to God in 2 Samuel 22? I ask this question with tongue in cheek, of course, but let us pursue it anyway, for the sake of argument. It would be almost impossible to overlook the fact that David acknowledges God's salvific power both at the chapter's beginning (2 Sam 22:1–20) and at its end (2 Sam 22:28–51). God is his fortress, his rock, and his shield (2 Sam 22:2–3), the one who saves him from his

> What kind of a song does David sing in chapter 22?

enemies at every turn (2 Sam 22:3–4, 18–19, 47–51). As an easily recognizable psalm of thanksgiving, the text expresses gratitude for the blessings David has hitherto received. At the poem's center, however, David explains the reason why God has favored him throughout his career. Incredibly, he claims that God rewards him "according to my righteousness" and "according to the purity of my hands" (2 Sam 22:21), as demonstrated by the fact that David has "kept the ways of the Lord" and has refrained from any "wrongdoing against God" (2 Sam 22:22). He also states that he has not disregarded any of God's statutes or laws (2 Sam 22:23), and that he remains patently "innocent" of any sin (2 Sam 22:24)! Therein lies the secret to his success: righteousness and purity before God (2 Sam 22:25). To a reader moving sequentially through the book of 2 Samuel (as opposed to the book of Psalms), these claims cannot avoid sticking in the throat. For if we have learned one thing about David's House to this point in the story, its catastrophic lack of "righteousness," "purity," and "innocence" generates a self-annihilating sword. David's dynasty has become a trainwreck, precisely because David raped Bathsheba and murdered Uriah. If God really does act "loyally with the loyal" as David supposes, "innocently with the innocent" and "with purity toward the pure," then we should expect God to "twist" (2 Sam 22:26–27) rather than to rubber-stamp the crooked man's political ambitions.

Who, me?, David seems to say. No, I never took advantage. I never pursued my own interests over yours. I never paced the roof. I never cheated and I never lied. I listened and obeyed; I loved and I served. I left nothing undone. Does he think God and the reader are blind? Does he believe his own lies? Has Israel's king become only more of the self-deluded narcissist that he always was (see 2 Sam 23:3–5)? Hard to dodge the conclusion that in conclusion, David sings a *Song of Myself*.

Reading from the textual outside in, 2 Samuel 22 cannot help but look like triumphalism. Some readers will therefore cook up excuses for David's audacity: "While we must admit that David sinned in chapter 11, his passionate faith seems to have outweighed that sin, which is why God gave him a second chance." This hermeneutical backflip winds up self-justifying the military victories for which David thanks God, and so buries the chapter's tension in a subtle oxymoron where it can be more easily ignored: ultimately, David's "gifts" are really (wink, wink) well-deserved rewards. The move to Manifest Destiny, American imperialism, and Christian nationalism follows closely behind. Other readers, however, when faced with the prospect of a violent David praising his equally violent God, will conjure up irony in order to preserve the poem's preachability within the well-educated, ethically sophisticated church. If the Old Testament's royal theology offends one's preexisting values and assumptions, simply debunk it and move on. David doesn't deserve his gifts after all, but the text (wink, wink) never actually supposes that he does.

Neither of these two options holds much water. Instead, the prophetic text poses a bedeviling riddle that can be answered only from the textual inside out. Inasmuch as the reader has been provoked into contemplating the mysterious interpenetration of Punishment and Promise throughout the preceding storyline, now he or she must wrestle with a new (and more pointed) version of the same puzzle. How does one make sense of a Song that has been placed on the lips of a man, who, by every legal metric, forfeits his right to sing it? If the book of 2 Samuel remains the reader's historical and mathematical soapbox, then the problem will attract only historical and mathematical solutions. Either David's words are justified or they aren't. But if the reader allows 2 Samuel to become his or her eviscerative crucifixion—a gut-ripping, soul-crushing impalement of the autonomous ego (see Matt 5:29–30)—then the paradox of chapter 22 may indeed serve that reader as a doorway into hope. Grace cannot be objectified, enumerated, categorized, and then pinned, like a dead beetle, to a card. It must be chewed, savored, and digested. It must be sung.

Can a tragic narrative depicting rape and murder (among numerous other atrocities) really be heard as a Song of Solomon (see 2 Sam 12:24–25)? Do the Former Prophets—for all their grotesque, dystopian chaos—present us with the gift of holy bread? Might Saul's suicide break the reader's heart on the Surgeon's operating table? Autonomous king that I am, will I yet find in these books' disturbing portraits of human waste an unlikely Pathway into worship? The Bible's prayer book has not been authored by a scoundrel who deserves my vilification, nor by a "hero of the faith" who merits my fanatical special pleading. On the contrary, 2 Samuel 22 consists of words prayed by a man like me. Thus I conclude: the House that God builds from David's dry bones is not a palace, but a hospital. It is a chapel for cheaters, a cathedral for the condemned.

> The House that God builds from David's dry bones is not a palace, but a hospital. It is a chapel for cheaters, and a cathedral for the condemned.

Worship and Waste

The last four chapters of 2 Samuel serve as a theological reflection on the book as a whole, with reference to 1 Samuel but with a particular focus on Punishment and Promise as these themes take center stage, especially after Saul has died. The unit compares well with Judges 17–21, which narrates a dischronologous set of meta-stories that summarize and comment upon the pattern of idolatry portrayed in Judges 1–16. Likewise, 2 Samuel 21–24 does not move the reader forward in time from 2 Samuel 20, but presents him or her with a selection of chiastically arranged, retrospective windows into the meaning of David's life. Two vignettes form the shell (2 Sam 21:1–14 and 24:1–25), memories about David's companions and their exploits fit within that (2 Sam 21:15–22 and 23:8–39), and finally, David's psalm and last words comprise the yolky center (2 Sam 22:1—23:7), whose core within the core portrays a David either insightfully or delusionally convinced of his sinlessness. Thus, the most important exegetical debate generated by this literary construction turns on the question of whether the implied author's Easter egg should be regarded as fresh or rotten. If we roll away the stone, will the murderer-rapist's tomb release a stench? What kind of man emerges in the book's final frames?

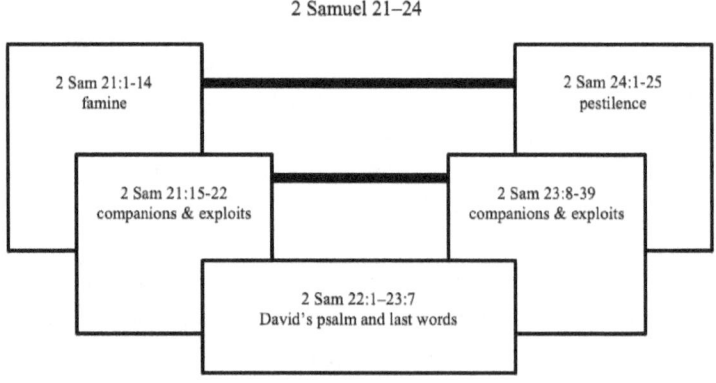

Among 2 Samuel's wide array of stained-glass images, its twenty-first and twenty-fourth chapters cast David in a priest-like role (see 2 Sam 6:13–15; 8:18). The first of these two stories begins with a famine for which David seeks out a remedy (2 Sam 21:1). Contemporary readers may become confused (and a bit disturbed) to find out that the text assigns Israel's

agricultural shortfall not to a natural fluctuation in climate, but to Saul's efforts to kill off as many Gibeonites as possible (2 Sam 21:1–2). Wait, what? Even if this explanation strikes one as plausible, Saul's bloodlust vis-à-vis the Gibeonites still pops off the page as totally new information, since no mention of it appears in the book of 1 Samuel. Moreover, when the Gibeonites call for the public "impaling" (2 Sam 21:6; see 21:9, 13) of seven, male descendants of Saul, the man after God's own heart issues no pushback whatsoever (2 Sam 21:3–6). Not only that, but the modern impulse to escape this story's moral embarrassment through irony (i.e., as another example of David acting badly) will struggle to make sense of its conclusion: "God was mollified with respect to the land after all this" (2 Sam 21:14). The ghastly crucifixion seems to work! Even if we were to invent a complicated backstory wherein the condemned House of Saul somehow robbed the Israelite populace of its food supply (an unlikely scenario at best), we would still need to admit that problems of food security are nowadays tackled through very different means. What could possibly be the point of such a weird and violent story? And how does it act as a theological window for readers who submit themselves to the book's prophetic knife?

The situation described in 2 Sam 21:1–14 embroils David in a tension between what will probably feel to the reader, when first considered, like mutually exclusive truths. Saul's dynasty is unquestionably doomed (see 1 Sam 13:14; 2 Sam 7:15). Nevertheless, David has sworn an oath to preserve and protect Jonathan's seed (see 1 Sam 20:16–17, 42; 2 Sam 9:1), which he maintains by sparing Mephibosheth in 2 Sam 21:7. Aware of this, the reader's eyes will probably glitch when he or she sees Mephibosheth's name listed on the roster of executed men in the very next verse (2 Sam 21:8). Logically, this second Mephibosheth must be a different person (i.e., a son of Rizpah) from the Mephibosheth who appears in chapters 4, 9, and 19. Nevertheless, the double-take that occurs because of the name's orthographic reduplication—even if it lasts for only a microsecond—presents a clue to the way in which Saul's dynastic tragedy mirrors and therefore informs one's perception of David's thorny crown. How do Punishment and Promise finally relate to one another? Does one concept simply outweigh the other, as if each contained a specific quantity of God-given mass and therefore exerted a greater or lesser gravitational pull? Do the two forces engage in a zero-sum contest for theological dominance from which only one winner can emerge? Is God trapped? Must he either renege on his vows or choose to ignore David's sin? Or does God quietly hide the Promise of 2 Samuel 7 inside David's shadowy "vale of tears" (see Ps 23:4)? On its own, 2 Sam 21:1-14 offers nothing like a complete answer to this question, but it does frame David's Song in 2 Samuel 22 with another funeral. Rizpah protects her children's bodies from birds and scavengers (2 Sam 21:10), David hears about her remarkable act of devotion (2 Sam 21:11), and in response, he organizes a proper interment for the whole, crumbling House (2 Sam 21:12-14). It's not so much that David does the right thing or the wrong thing in this difficult-to-understand story, nor that the reader should go and do likewise (even if that were possible), but that Israel's priest-king inhabits the uneasy space between one Mephibosheth's crucifixion and another Mephibosheth's resurrection. For the prophetically-minded reader, these realities prove to be "one in the same" (an intentional eggcorn, by the way). Impalement on 2 Samuel's textual tree becomes a rhetorical doorway into new life.

At the other end of the book's concluding chiasm, David makes the mistake of carrying out a military census—the sort of thing an Assyrian or Babylonian emperor would do to prepare for new conquests (2 Sam 24:1-9). Upon further review of his actions, however, he admits his sin (2 Sam 24:10; see 24:17), echoing 2 Sam 12:13. Thus David remains 2 Samuel's archetypal Man to the bitter end (see 2 Sam 12:7)—sinners do not transcend their human nature and confession never goes out of style. Meanwhile, the implied author's careful word choice suggests several intertextual connections that help the reader to understand this meta-story's function as additional commentary on the overall book. For example, David recognizes the "foolishness" (2 Sam 24:10) of his actions. Previously he used this word when asking God to "make foolish" Ahitophel's advice (2 Sam 15:31). Stone the stones, prayed David; curse the curse; turn the Punishment inside out. "Cross out" my sin once more (2 Sam 24:10; see 12:13).

Crucially, when granting this request, God does *not* magically nullify the judgment that David faces (2 Sam 24:12-13), as if divine forgiveness simply possessed more teeth than David's sin and therefore gets the better of its weaker adversary in a tussle. Rather, like Sheba's severed head, David flies over Zion's battlements and plunges into darkness (2 Sam 24:14). The only thing he can do in response to his mistake—the only thing that any sinner who has wasted his or her life can do—is to fall hard on worship (2 Sam 24:14-25). If 2 Sam 21:1-14 sets David within the difficult tension that plagues another man's dynasty, 2 Sam 24:1-25 shows the reader yet again that the same problem applies also to David's ruined House. Because of his ambition, an appalling seventy-seven thousand more bodies are added to the stack (2 Sam 24:15)! Even now, the corpse-ridden book of 2 Samuel never stops boiling over with sorrow, tears, and pain. David's Israel has been threshed; it has paid sin's gruesome price (2 Sam 24:25). For this reason, the hope that David personifies does not equate to a get-out-of-jail-free card, for grace never was a "second chance to do the right thing." Rather, his character becomes for the reader a dusty, concrete floor at the bottom of a twelve-step staircase. He is a naked dancer, a barefoot refugee, and a "dead dog" (see 1 Sam 24:14) in search of transformation. He is a failed father who needs a little mercy now. Peace, peace, proclaims the narrator—"peace of Christ" where there was no peace before (2 Sam 24:25).

☩

Whatever the particular circumstances that surround a divorce, and whether the decision may be judged as a good or bad, one cannot avoid the sense of loss that pervades the dissolution of a once-happy marriage. We had very few material assets to split—nothing much beyond the wedding China, a beat-up Honda, and our student loans. Still, the dead bodies piled up. Such a strange thing to wake up one day counting the dozens of family friends and relatives whom I would probably never see or talk to again, living in various places I would never revisit and in homes I would never reenter. I had spent the last decade of my life deep within an extended network that would instinctively preserve its relationship with her and not with me. It was only natural, even if *she* had pulled the plug, leaving *me* to bury our figurative child at court. In the absence of a Solomonic sword, how could they possibly adjudicate our case, anyway? Like a sudden crash in the market, years of relational investment evaporated overnight. I loved my former in-laws, and I had expected to join my ex-wife in caring for them in their old age. I looked forward to our holidays together and to our mountain retreats. I enjoyed their quirks and fussy habits. Yet despite my wishes, and in my former mother-in-law's own words, I had somehow changed from an "adopted son" into a "good friend"—a "good friend" with whom she no longer speaks.

They tell me that I should appreciate the laughter and the memories while endeavoring to "make some new ones." I suppose such advice is wise, in its own way, but I notice that the Ivy Leaguers who offer it usually possess little insight into the waste itself. Yes, good times were had along the way, but nothing of what I had tried so hard to construct wound up accruing to the future. The loans have been paid, the car has been sold, and most of the China—what's left of it—has chipped. Surely I am like grass, and all my glory is like a flower of the field. The unforgiving, Saskatchewan winter folds every leaf and petal under a snowbank, where they eventually dissolve in the spring melt. The song I used to sing has flown away south.

Whatever these gurus' good intentions, their recommendation to "make some new ones" feels to me like a recommendation to "rebuild." I am suspicious. If the manufacture of my own house didn't work the first time around, why should it work now? True wisdom has to do with accepting God's movement in the dark. The way of the Cross is the way of the compost pile.

> The way of the Cross is the way of the compost pile.

When our daughters were born in the years following remarriage, my second wife and I wanted names for each that expressed our joy beyond the sorrow. "Abigail Eleanor" came first—"My Father Rejoices" in the "Light." Nineteen months later, I cupped my hand over another baby's soft scalp and called her "Susannah Wren," with a nod to Luke 12:22–31. Not a stitch of clothing on that tiny, naked body, but Solomon in all his splendor never dressed as magnificently as she. Then we held her tight and cried, cried, cried away the pain. These days, Susie's delightful aphorisms regularly trump her culture's sage advice. "Mommy, did you know that God is food?" and "Daddy, a closed church is just *silly*." No, our family's flower-bird doesn't seem to worry too much about stocking her barn, building her house, or being awesome to please the Man. She sings a wiser song. So I will follow her lead—what have I got to lose? I will fall hard on worship, for the "F"s have set me Free.

☩

One layer inside the chiasm's shell, 2 Sam 21:15–22 and 23:8–39 ask the reader to reconsider David's larger-than-life reputation. These two passages paint a picture of strength, success, honor, and victory. No matter how unlikeable David's overall persona may be to modern democrats, here he is no villain. At the same time, however, the text also resists any notion of a Sunday-school hero, patronizingly whitewashed in order to cultivate the reader's virtue. The devil's in the details, as usual. Chapter 21 remembers a series of four, Philistine giants who "fell at the hand of David and his servants" (2 Sam 21:22). If Goliath's name rings a bell (and who could forget 1 Samuel 17?), the reader may imagine David leading the charge against all four, but the preceding verses do not agree. Unlike the red-haired boy who once angled for a military and theological showdown with Israel's enemies, the David of 2 Samuel 21 becomes surprisingly "weary" from the get-go (2 Sam 21:15). In fact, this David would not have survived his wars at all if his Mighty-Men had not intervened (2 Sam 21:16–17). The son of Jesse may have risen to the top of Israel's political hierarchy, but as far as 2 Sam 21:15–22 is concerned, his dependence stands out as the thing to remember. Even his victory over Goliath—David's most famous exploit of all—the text quietly reassigns to someone else (2 Sam 21:19). Again, it's not so much that David does the right thing or the wrong thing in this mind-bending alternative to 1 Samuel 17, nor that the reader should go and do likewise. Rather, the broken man who personifies 2 Samuel's hope gets what the Law tells us he deserves (i.e., dynastic ruin), only to find out that what he deserves is something like being tossed, with a millstone around his neck, into an ocean of providential love.

If 2 Samuel 21 muddies the memory of David's legendary awesomeness, 2 Sam 23:8–39 makes a similar move by means of a different tactic. Again the reader encounters a collection of heroic exploits undertaken by David's followers. These images cast him less as a dependent, however, and more as a magnetic leader, someone renowned for his unflagging strength and charisma. David never shies away from danger and he never backs down (see 2 Sam 21:9–10); he publicly appreciates the bravery with which he is surrounded and on which his enfranchised position relies (2 Sam 23:15–17). But when the reader finally comes to the last name on David's roster of loyal supporters (2 Sam 23:39), the hero's winning personality suddenly flips upside down and inside out. For the text does not omit Bathsheba's dead husband from its scriptural hall of fame, though it certainly could have if the implied author had so desired. Like a penny buried in cake, Uriah remains the eternal victim of his Davidic king's greed (cf. Matt 10:4; Mark 3:19; Luke 6:16), while David himself remains alive to enjoy the fruits of God's favor. Jesse's son gets what he deserves in the book of 2 Samuel if and only if mercy sums up the Law's purpose from the start.

"The act of ruling humanity with righteousness and the fear of God," observes David, "is like morning sunshine, a morning without clouds" (2 Sam 23:3–4). And that's pretty much the sum of it—that's the story of my godly House and its everlasting Promise, in contrast to all the "worthless" (see 2 Sam 16:7; 20:1) scoundrels headed for destruction (2 Sam 23:5–7). Really, David? How can this statement possibly bear up when night after night, the buzzy, neon sign above your headboard blinks the name of Uriah into Jerusalem's dark alleyways and lonely streets? What are we to make of your outrageous claims? What kind of a song do you finally sing?

From the perspective of a moral mathematician, David will never escape the accusation of self-conceit. After all, the book's form and content simply do not permit its reader to accept the poetry at the core of its conclusion without also reflecting on David's mistakes. Both the chiasm's shell and its corresponding "white" prohibit a posture of naïve credulity toward David's drippy yolk. At the same time, if the last four chapters of 2 Samuel were designed to drop an ironic bomb on the Bible's royal theology once and for all, I can imagine numerous alternative conclusions to David's story that would get the job done with more efficiency and with less ambiguity. The key to 2 Samuel 22 is the readerly recognition that David's poem (irrespective of the historical king's probable psychology) emerges from the interior universe of a sublime, theological mystery. His words become a textual sanctuary, a walled Garden that proves far larger on the inside than it first appears from without. The psalm makes sense only from within the topsy-turvy, counterintuitive world of Scripture, a Land of eternal Promise where gifts are real, where grace happens, and where $2 - 1 = 3$.

David makes a Law-full calculation in chapter 22, and I will be the first to admit that on its surface, the king's arithmetic collapses in on itself: "I have acted rightly," he claims, "and God has granted me the fruits of my right behavior" (2 Sam 21:21–27). This idea sums up great swaths of both Deuteronomy and Proverbs. Virtue generates a reward; tangible reward therefore signals a person's underlying virtue. That said, Moses, Jeremiah, and Jesus all agree on the teleology of divine Law—in the end, it functions to break the lawyer's heart (Deut 30:1–6; Jer 31:31–34; Matt 5:29–30). In other words, the Law "works" only when we admit our inability to keep it. Thus, the only condition in which David can legitimately appeal to Moses's math without transgressing the first and second commandments is one of abject failure, marked by the admission that his life has become a magnificent waste. But then, if he has failed so miserably, how does the Law's calculus—predicated on the lawyer's virtue—continue to support his weight?

Only a *worshiper* can read 2 Samuel 22 without either disgust or special pleading, for only a worshiper can know that within Solomon's love Song, God has embedded the strange gift of nakedness and defeat, while within nakedness and defeat lie endless fractals of adoration and loss, adoration and loss for which no words I know suffice. I give myself to God because of what I have been given; I give back to God again all that God first gave me. I accomplish exactly nothing through this cyclical act of exchange. Nothing ever gets done. Nothing is ever achieved. In the same way, when Mother Teresa famously listened to God, God listened right back. To any culture trained on military victories and zero sums, such imaginary discourse will seem a colossal waste of breath. But such worship is just the sort of waste that our heartsick world needs most—a crooked trail that leads the sinner out of his or her manufactured hell and into God's paradoxical economy of grace (see Hos 14:1–3). Here at last, in the book's final frames, David appears to the reader not as a loser, but as a true Winner, for he has "crossed into" and "passed through" the world's unquenchable thirst for war.

> Only a worshiper can know that within Solomon's love Song, God has embedded the strange gift of nakedness and defeat.

Can murderers and rapists sing Israel's irrational Song of Solomon? Can tyrants and thieves recite it? Can a ruined House find within its suffering the durable Promises of God? Yes, yes, yes.

Postlude

George Herbert turns his reader's attention to the Floor. He asks me to register in myself what has always proven most difficult to admit, that the foundation underneath my awesome archways remains dusty and "checkered all along." Yet I am neither honest enough nor modest enough to do what Herbert says. I need help. I need a Physician whose scalpel is sharp enough to cut the parasitic Snake from my heart. For that reason, I am grateful to the unnamed, west-Asian, premodern Israelites who, when every other culture of the ancient world had doubled down on its Songs of Self, possessed enough humility to craft from their most cherished, national memories a textual dagger that could perform the prophetic operation I require.

The book of 2 Samuel is a theological tragedy, sleek and sharp like a knife. That's no surprise, given its canonical situation within a series of other tragedies that slowly tell the story of a people unable to keep the Land it had been Promised. Everything slips away in the end: the kingship, the castle, and the court; the music, the melodies, and the admirers; the wealth, the women, and the wine. No more milk; no more honey. By the rivers of Babylon, we hung up our harps (Ps 137:1–3). Anguish replaces laughter; tears flow from the widow's empty jar. In the Old Testament, there is simply no shortcut, no trick play, by which to avoid lament. All roads lead down from the Temple, across the Kidron Valley, through the Garden of Gethsemane, and up the Olive Mount. The Achilles rupture itself struck me mainly as an inconvenience. The real pain set in only when the doctor cut open my leg, uncoiled the tendon, and laced it back together again. Surgery hurts.

Postlude

Hither sometimes Sin steals, and stains
The marble's neat and curious veins:
But all is cleansed when the marble weeps.
Sometimes Death, puffing at the door,
Blows all the dust about the floor:
But while he thinks to spoil the room, he sweeps.

In the weeks following my hospital visit, I found myself at home, in bed, with a giant boot strapped to my right leg. I spent my afternoons getting chubby on too much ice cream and my nights writhing around in search of another oxycodone. Meanwhile, my wife worked, and then worked again until she dropped, cooking dinners and loading the dishwasher, doing the laundry and sweeping the floors. The whole experience proved an uncomfortable, creaturely foretaste of my inevitable death. I had become a temporary cripple, and I didn't like it one bit. I wanted to walk again—as soon as possible—if only to feel less like a dependent child and more like a husband, a father, and a man. *Egō ho anthrōpos. Ani ha'ish.*

My daughter Abigail, who was not quite three years old at the time, quickly realized that something had gone seriously wrong with her daddy, for our normal routines around the house had turned upside down and inside out. So she brought all her coloring books and crayons to my bedside, clambered into my lap, and spent her mornings creating one ridiculous piece of artwork after another while chatting off my ears. Little did she know how deeply I appreciated her concern. Little did she know that as she colored rainbows and prattled on about princesses, I was falling in love with her all over again.

I have read Herbert's poem hundreds of times now, usually doing so while caught up in its tortured intuition for irony. Rereading it now, with my daughters in mind, I am surprised (though I really shouldn't be) to find myself laughing out loud. How could I have missed its absurd humor? Huffing and puffing at the door, and with every intention to "spoil the room," Death transforms into the church's maid and butler! Tragedy turns into comedy; 2 − 1 = 3. David's Savior always was and always will be David's resurrected Son.

> David's Savior always was and always will be David's resurrected Son.

Before you go, and while the Old Testament's narrative Prophets hold your attention for one more wasted breath, consider yourself a flower of the field. Learn to pray like Susannah Wren. A self-possessed church is just *silly*.

Endnotes

1. Michelangelo di Lodovico Buonarroti Simoni, *David* (c. 1501–1504), marble sculpture, 517 cm x 199 cm, Galleria dell'Accademia, Florence, Italy, https://en.wikipedia.org/wiki/David_(Michelangelo)#/media/File:'David'_by_Michelangelo_Fir_JBU004.jpg. This image was created by Jörg Bittner Unna and has been reproduced under the Creative Commons Attribution-ShareAlike 3.0 International license: https://creativecommons.org/licenses/by-sa/3.0/.

2. Billy Joel, "Only the Good Die Young" (1978).

3. C. S. Lewis, *The Lion, The Witch, and the Wardrobe*, 158.

4. See Robert France, "An Infinity of Waste—The Brutal Reality of the First World War" (November 8, 2018), https://theconversation.com/an-infinity-of-waste-the-brutal-reality-of-the-first-world-war-106593.

5. DataMasters, "Tips and Tricks for Finding and Marketing to Corvette Owners" (accessed April 27, 2024), https://www.datamasters.org/corvette-owners/#:~:text=Demographics%20for%20Corvette%20Owners&text=The%20largest%20age%20group%20(12,nearly%2055%25%20of%20sales).

6. Walt Whitman, *Song of Myself* (1892), 52.3, first appearing as an untitled poem in the self-published volume *Leaves of Grass* (1855).

7. Sarah Vowell, *Take the Cannoli: Stories from the New World*, read by the author on *This American Life*, https://www.thisamericanlife.org/54/transcript.

8. Bono, *Surrender: 40 Songs, One Story*, 342.

9. Edward Hopper, *Nighthawks* (1942), oil on canvas, 84.1 cm x 152.4 cm, Art Institute of Chicago, Chicago, Illinois, https://en.wikipedia.org/wiki/Nighthawks_(Hopper)#/media/File:Nighthawks_by_Edward_Hopper_1942.jpg. This image is in the public domain.

10. Whit Stillman (director), *The Last Days of Disco* (1998).

11. R. A. Carlson, *David, The Chosen King: A Traditio-Historical Approach to the Second Book of Samuel*.

Endnotes

12. David M. Gunn, *The Story of King David: Genre and Interpretation*, 94–111 (95).

13. BibleProject, "2 Samuel" (March 26, 2016), https://bibleproject.com/explore/video/2-samuel/.

14. William Shakespeare, *The Life of Henry the Fifth*, 3.1.1.

15. William Shakespeare, *The Life of Henry the Fifth*, 3.1.5–6.

16. Photographer unknown, "All Enmity Forgotten" (1913), photograph (gelatin silver print), 12 cm x 13 cm, US Library of Congress, Washington, DC, https://www.loc.gov/resource/ppmsca.58170/. This image is in the public domain.

17. Mary Gauthier, "Mercy Now" (2005).

18. Mary Gauthier, "Mercy Now" (2005).

19. William Shakespeare, *Much Ado About Nothing*, 2.3.61–63.

20. George Frideric Handel, *Messiah* (1741).

21. See Sara Koenig, *Bathsheba Survives*, 8.

22. Jean-Léon Gérôme, *Bethsabée* (1889), oil on canvas, 60.5 cm x 100 cm, private collection, https://en.wikipedia.org/wiki/Bathsheba_(G%C3%A9r%C3%B4me)#/media/File:Bethsab%C3%A9e,_by_Jean-L%C3%A9on_G%C3%A9r%C3%B4me.jpg. This image is in the public domain.

23. Sara Koenig, *Bathsheba Survives*, 66.

24. Sara Koenig, *Bathsheba Survives*, 74 (citing Erasmus, *Collected Works*).

25. Jean Bourdichon, *Bathsheba Bathing*, in *The Book of the Hours of Louis XII* (c. 1498–99), tempera and gold, 24.3 cm x 17 cm, J. Paul Getty Museum, Los Angeles, California, https://www.getty.edu/art/collection/object/1096SE. This image is in the public domain.

26. C. S. Lewis, *The Lion, The Witch, and the Wardrobe*, 148.

27. Jean-Léon Gérôme, *La Naissance de Vénus* (1890), oil on canvas, 129.5 cm x 79.5 cm, private collection, https://en.wikipedia.org/wiki/The_Birth_of_Venus_(G%C3%A9r%C3%B4me)#/media/File:Gerome_venus.jpg. This image is in the public domain.

28. George Herbert, *Love (3)* (1633).

29. C. S. Lewis, *The Lion, The Witch, and the Wardrobe*, 144.

30. Ian Morgan Cron and Suzanne Stabile, *The Road Back to You: An Enneagram Journey to Self-Discovery*.

31. The story of Archimedes's discovery regarding water displacement first appears in a Roman architectural treatise written by Vitruvius (c. 30–20 BC) and is widely known. For further information, see Wikipedia, "Archimedes," https://en.wikipedia.org/wiki/Archimedes, as well as various, embedded hyperlinks that also pertain.

Endnotes

32. For example, see Walter Brueggemann, *Solomon: Israel's Ironic Icon of Human Achievement*.

33. Gustav Klimt, *The Kiss* (1907–8), oil and gold leaf on canvas, 180 cm x 180 cm, Österreichische Galerie Belvedere, Vienna, Austria, https://en.wikipedia.org/wiki/The_Kiss_(Klimt)#/media/File:The_Kiss_-_Gustav_Klimt_-_Google_Cultural_Institute.jpg. This image is in the public domain.

34. For example, see David Shepherd, *King David: Innocent Blood and Bloodguilt*, 150–51.

35. John Newton, "Pensive, Doubting, Fearful Heart" (1779).

36. John Newton, "Pensive, Doubting, Fearful Heart" (1779).

37. Giovanni Canavesio, *The Suicide of Judas* (1491), fresco, Notre-Dame des Fontaines, La Brigue, France, https://en.wikipedia.org/wiki/Giovanni_Canavesio#/media/File:Der_geh%C3%A4ngte_Judas.jpg. This image is in the public domain.

38. For example, see Keith Bodner, *David Observed: A King in the Eyes of His Court*, 124–39.

39. James Tissot, *La mort d'Absalon* (c. 1896–1902), Gouache on board, 27.1 × 14 cm, Jewish Museum, New York, New York, https://thejewishmuseum.org/collection/26542-the-death-of-absalom-la-mort-d-absalon. This image is in the public domain.

40. In Hebrew texts, 2 Sam 18:33—19:43 is numbered 2 Sam 19:1–44.

41. St. Paul's Cathedral Nave, London (2014), photo, https://en.wikipedia.org/wiki/File:St_Paul%27s_Cathedral_Nave,_London,_UK_-_Diliff.jpg. This image was created by David Iliff and has been reproduced under the Creative Commons Attribution-ShareAlike 3.0 International license: https://creativecommons.org/licenses/by-sa/3.0/.

42. Walt Whitman, *Song of Myself*, 52.1–3.

43. Katy Perry, "Roar" (2013).

44. Whit Stillman (director), *The Last Days of Disco* (1998).

45. See Walter Brueggemann, "2 Samuel 21–24: An Appendix of Deconstruction?," 383–97.

Bibliography

Ackroyd, Peter R. "The Succession Narrative (So-Called)." *Interpretation* 35 (1981) 383–96.
Alter, Robert. *The Art of Biblical Narrative*. 2nd ed. New York: Basic, 2011.
———. *The David Story: A Translation with Commentary of 1 and 2 Samuel*. New York: Norton, 1999.
Anderson, A. A. *2 Samuel*. Word Biblical Commentary 11. Dallas: Word, 1989.
Arnold, Bill T. "The Amalekite's Report of Saul's Death: Political Intrigue or Incompatible Sources?" *JETS* 32 (1989) 289–98.
Auld, A. Graeme. *I & II Samuel: A Commentary*. Old Testament Library. Louisville: Westminster John Knox, 2011.
Avioz, Michael. "The Motif of Beauty in the Books of Samuel and Kings." *VT* 59 (2009) 341–59.
Bailey, Randall C. *David in Love and War: The Pursuit of Power in 2 Samuel 10–12*. Journal for the Study of the Old Testament Supplement Series 75. Sheffield: Sheffield Academic, 1990.
Bar-Efrat, Shimon. *Narrative Art in the Bible*. London: T&T Clark International, 2004.
Barron, Robert. *2 Samuel*. Brazos Theological Commentary on the Bible. Grand Rapids: Brazos, 2015.
Berger, Yitzhak. "On Patterning in the Book of Samuel: 'News of Death' and the Kingship of David." *Journal for the Study of the Old Testament* 35 (2011) 463–81.
BibleProject. "2 Samuel." https://bibleproject.com/explore/video/2-samuel/.
Birch, Bruce C. "The First and Second Books of Samuel." In *The New Interpreter's Bible*, edited by Leander E. Keck, 2:947–1383. Nashville: Abingdon, 1998.
Blenkinsopp, Joseph. "Another Contribution to the Succession Narrative Debate (2 Samuel 11–20; 1 Kings 1–2)." *Journal for the Study of the Old Testament* 38 (2013) 35–58.
———. *David Remembered: Kingship and National Identity in Ancient Israel*. Grand Rapids: Eerdmans, 2013.
Bodner, Keith. *David Observed: A King in the Eyes of His Court*. Hebrew Bible Monographs 5. Sheffield: Sheffield Phoenix, 2008.
———. *The Rebellion of Absalom*. London: Routledge, 2014.
Bono. *Surrender: 40 Songs, One Story*. New York: Knopf, 2022.
Borgman, Paul. *David, Saul, and God: Rediscovering an Ancient Story*. Oxford: Oxford University Press, 2008.
Bosworth, David. "Evaluating King David: Old Problems and Recent Scholarship." *Catholic Biblical Quarterly* 68 (2006) 191–210.

Bibliography

Bowman, Richard G. "The Complexity of Character and the Ethics of Complexity: The Case of King David." In *Character and Scripture: Moral Formation, Community, and Biblical Interpretation*, edited by William P. Brown, 73–97. Grand Rapids: Eerdmans, 2002.

Brueggemann, Walter. "2 Samuel 21–24: An Appendix of Deconstruction?" *Catholic Biblical Quarterly* 50 (1988) 383–97.

———. *David and His Theologian: Literary, Social, and Theological Investigations of the Early Monarchy*. Edited by K. C. Hanson. Eugene, OR: Cascade, 2011.

———. *David's Truth in Israel's Imagination and Memory*. Minneapolis: Fortress, 1985.

———. *First and Second Samuel*. Interpretation: A Bible Commentary for Teaching and Preaching. Louisville: John Knox, 1990.

———. *Solomon: Israel's Ironic Icon of Human Achievement*. Columbia: University of South Carolina Press, 2005.

Campbell, Antony F. *2 Samuel*. Forms of the Old Testament Literature 8. Grand Rapids: Eerdmans, 2005.

———. "2 Samuel 21–24: The Enigma Factor." In *For and Against David: Story and History in the Books of Samuel*, edited by A. Graeme Auld and Erik Eynikel, 347–58. Bibliotheca Ephemeridum Theologicarum Lovaniensium 232. Leuven: Peeters, 2010.

Capek, Filip. "David's Ambiguous Testament in 1 Kings 2:1–12 and the Role of Joab in the Succession Narrative." *Communio viatorum* 52 (2010) 4–26.

Carlson, R. A. *David, the Chosen King: A Traditio-Historical Approach to the Second Book of Samuel*. Translated by Eric J. Sharpe and Stanley Rudman. Stockholm: Almqvist & Wiksell, 1964.

Chapman, Stephen B. *1 Samuel as Christian Scripture: A Theological Commentary*. Grand Rapids: Eerdmans, 2016.

———. "Rizpah, Mother of Sorrows." *Bible Today* 62 (2024) 263–68.

Chavel, Simeon. "Compositry and Creativity in 2 Sam 21:1–14." *JBL* 122 (2003) 23–52.

Clines, David J. A., and Tamara C. Eskenazi. *Telling Queen Michal's Story: An Experiment in Comparative Interpretation*. Journal for the Study of the Old Testament Supplement Series 119. Sheffield: Sheffield Academic, 1991.

Conroy, Charles. *Absalom Absalom! Narrative and Language in 2 Sam 13–20*. Analecta Biblica 81. Rome: Biblical Institute, 1978.

Cron, Ian Morgan, and Suzanne Stabile. *The Road Back to You: An Enneagram Journey to Self-Discovery*. Downers Grove, IL: InterVarsity, 2016.

Damrosch, David. *The Narrative Covenant: Transformations of Genre in the Growth of Biblical Literature*. San Francisco: Harper & Row, 1987.

Edenburg, Cynthia, and Juha Pakkala, eds. *Is Samuel Among the Deuteronomists? Current Views on the Place of Samuel in a Deuteronomistic History*. Ancient Israel and Its Literature 16. Atlanta: SBL, 2013.

Eslinger, Lyle. *House of God or House of David: The Rhetoric of 2 Samuel 7*. Journal for the Study of the Old Testament Supplement Series 164. Sheffield: Sheffield Academic, 1994.

Exum, J. Cheryl. "Rizpah." *Word & World* 17 (1997) 260–68.

Firth, David G. *1 & 2 Samuel*. Apollos Old Testament Commentary 8. Downers Grove, IL: InterVarsity, 2009.

———. "Shining the Lamp: The Rhetoric of 2 Samuel 5–24." *Tyndale Bulletin* 52 (2001) 203–24.

Bibliography

Flanagan, James W. "Court History or Succession Document? A Study of 2 Samuel 9–20 and 1 Kings 1–2." *JBL* 91 (1972) 172–81.

Fokkelman, J. P. *Narrative Art and Poetry in the Books of Samuel.* Vol. I, *King David (II Sam. 9–20 & 1 Kings 1–2).* Studia Semitica Neerlandica 20. Assen: Van Gorcum, 1981.

———. *Narrative Art and Poetry in the Books of Samuel.* Vol. II, *The Crossing Fates (I Sam. 13–31 and II Sam. 1).* Studia Semitica Neerlandica 23. Assen: Van Gorcum, 1986.

———. *Narrative Art and Poetry in the Books of Samuel.* Vol. III, *Throne and City (II Sam. 2–8 and 21–24).* Studia Semitica Neerlandica 27. Assen: Van Gorcum, 1986.

Frolov, Serge. "Succession Narrative: A 'Document' or a Phantom?" *JBL* 121 (2002) 81–104.

Frontain, Raymond-Jean, and Jan Wojcik, eds. *The David Myth in Western Literature.* West Lafayette, IN: Purdue University Press, 1980.

Gerbrandt, Gerald Eddie. *Kingship According to the Deuteronomistic History.* Society of Biblical Literature Dissertation Series 87. Atlanta: Scholars, 1986.

Gilmour, Rachelle. *Representing the Past: A Literary Analysis of Narrative Historiography in the Book of Samuel.* Supplements to Vetus Testamentum 143. Leiden: Brill, 2011.

Gordon, Robert P. *I & II Samuel: A Commentary.* Library of Biblical Interpretation. Grand Rapids: Zondervan, 1986.

Gros Louis, Kenneth R. R. "The Difficulty of Ruling Well: King David of Israel." *Semeia* 8 (1977) 15–33.

Gunn, David M. *The Story of King David: Genre and Interpretation.* Journal for the Study of the Old Testament Supplement Series 6. Sheffield: JSOT, 1978.

Hagan, Harry. "Deception as Motif and Theme in 2 Sm 9–20; 1 Kgs 1–2." *Biblica* 60 (1979) 301–26.

Halpern, Baruch. *David's Secret Demons: Messiah, Murderer, Traitor, King.* The Bible in Its World. Grand Rapids: Eerdmans, 2001.

Hamilton, James M. "The Typology of David's Rise to Power: Messianic Patterns in the Book of Samuel." *Southern Baptist Journal of Theology* 16 (2012) 4–25.

Herbert, George. *The Complete English Poems.* Edited by John Tobin. London: Penguin, 1991.

Hertzberg, Hans Wilhelm. *I & II Samuel: A Commentary.* Old Testament Library. Philadelphia: Westminster, 1964.

Juel, Donald. *Messianic Exegesis: Christological Interpretation of the Old Testament in Early Christianity.* Philadelphia: Fortress, 1988.

Keys, Gillian. *The Wages of Sin: A Reappraisal of "Succession Narrative."* Journal for the Study of the Old Testament Supplement Series 221. Sheffield: Sheffield Academic, 1996.

Klement, Herbert H. *II Samuel 21–24: Context, Structure and Meaning in the Samuel Conclusion.* European University Studies 23:682. Frankfurt am Main: Lang, 2000.

Koenig, Sara. *Bathsheba Survives.* Studies on Personalities of the Old Testament. Columbia: University of South Carolina Press, 2018.

Lasine, Stuart. "Judicial Narratives and the Ethics of Reading: The Reader as Judge of the Dispute Between Mephibosheth and Ziba." *Hebrew Studies* 30 (1989) 49–69.

Leithart, Peter J. *A Son to Me: An Exposition of 1 & 2 Samuel.* Moscow, ID: Canon, 2003.

Lewis, C. S. *The Lion, The Witch and the Wardrobe.* London: Puffin, 1967.

Linafelt, Tod. "Private Poetry and Public Eloquence in 2 Samuel 1:17–27: Hearing and Overhearing David's Lament for Jonathan and Saul." *Journal of Religion* 88 (2008) 497–526.

Linafelt, Tod, et al., eds. *The Fate of King David: The Past and Present of a Biblical Icon.* The Library of Hebrew Bible/Old Testament Studies 500. London: T&T Clark, 2010.

McCarter, P. Kyle, Jr. *II Samuel: A New Translation with Introduction, Notes and Commentary.* Anchor Bible 9. Garden City, NY: Doubleday, 1984.

———. "The Apology of David." *Journal of Biblical Literature* 99 (1980) 489–504.

———. "The Historical David." *Interpretation* 40 (1986) 117–29.

———. "'Plots, True or False': The Succession Narrative as Court Apologetic." *Interpretation* 35 (1981) 355–67.

McCarthy, Dennis J. "II Samuel 7 and the Structure of the Deuteronomic History." *Journal of Biblical Literature* 84 (1965) 131–38.

McKenzie, Steven L. "The So-Called Succession Narrative in the Deuteronomistic History." In *Die sogenannte Thronfolgegeschichte Davids: Neue Einsichten und Anfragen*, edited by Albert de Pury, 123–35. Orbis Biblicus et Orientalis 176. Göttingen: Vandenhoeck & Ruprecht, 2000.

———. "Why Didn't God Let David Build the Temple? The History of a Biblical Tradition." In *Worship and the Hebrew Bible: Essays in Honour of John T. Willis*, edited by M. Patrick Graham et al., 204–24. Journal for the Study of the Old Testament Supplement Series 284. Sheffield: Sheffield Academic, 1999.

Mettinger, Tryggve N. D. *King and Messiah: The Civil and Sacral Legitimation of the Israelite Kings.* Coniectanea Biblica: Old Testament Series 8. Lund: CWK Gleerup, 1976.

Morrison, Craig E. *2 Samuel.* Berit Olam: Studies in Hebrew Narrative & Poetry. Collegeville, MN: Liturgical, 2013.

Noth, Martin. *The Deuteronomistic History.* Journal for the Study of the Old Testament Supplement Series 15. Sheffield: JSOT, 1981.

O'Kane, Martin. "The Biblical King David and His Artistic and Literary Afterlives." *Biblical Interpretation* 6 (1998) 313–47.

Perdue, Leo G. "'Is There Anyone Left of the House of Saul': Ambiguity and the Characterization of David in the Succession Narrative." *Journal for the Study of the Old Testament* 9.30 (1984) 67–84.

Perry, Menakhem, and Meir Sternberg. "The King Through Ironic Eyes: Biblical Narrative and the Literary Reading Process." *Poetics Today* 7 (1986) 275–322.

Petersen, David L. "Portraits of David Canonical and Otherwise." *Interpretation* 40 (1986) 130–42.

Peterson, Eugene H. *First and Second Samuel.* Westminster Bible Companion. Louisville: Westminster John Knox, 1999.

Polzin, Robert. *David and the Deuteronomist: A Literary Study of the Deuteronomic History: Part Three, 2 Samuel.* Bloomington: Indiana University Press, 1993.

Provan, Iain W. "On 'Seeing' the Trees While Missing the Forest: The Wisdom of Characters and Readers in 2 Samuel and 1 Kings." In *In Search of True Wisdom: Essays in Old Testament Interpretation in Honour of Ronald E. Clements*, edited by Edward Ball, 153–73. Journal for the Study of the Old Testament Supplement Series 300. Sheffield: Sheffield Academic, 1999.

Bibliography

Roberts, J. J. M. "In Defense of the Monarchy: The Contribution of Israelite Kingship to Biblical Theology." In *Ancient Israelite Religion: Essays in Honor of Frank Moore Cross*, edited by Patrick D. Miller et al., 377–96. Philadelphia: Fortress, 1987.

Römer, Thomas C. *The So-Called Deuteronomistic History: A Sociological, Historical and Literary Introduction*. London: T&T Clark, 2005.

Rost, Leonhard. *The Succession to the Throne of David*. Translated by Michael D. Rutter and David M. Gunn. Historic Texts and Interpreters in Biblical Scholarship 1. Sheffield: Almond, 1982.

Satterthwaite, Philip E. "David in the Books of Samuel: A Messianic Hope?" In *The Lord's Anointed: Interpretation of Old Testament Messianic Texts*, edited by Philip E. Satterthwaite et al., 41–65. Tyndale House Studies. Carlisle: Paternoster, 1995.

Schulz, Alfons. "Narrative Art in the Books of Samuel." In *Narrative and Novella in Samuel: Studies by Hugo Gressmann and Other Scholars, 1906–1923*, edited by David M. Gunn, translated by David E. Orton, 119–70. Sheffield: Almond, 1991.

Shakespeare, William. *The Life of Henry the Fifth*. In *The Yale Shakespeare: The Complete Works*, edited by Wilbur L. Cross and Tucker Brooke, 767–807. New York: Barnes & Noble, 1993.

———. *Much Ado About Nothing*. In *The Yale Shakespeare: The Complete Works*, edited by Wilbur L. Cross and Tucker Brooke, 221–50. New York: Barnes & Noble, 1993.

Shepherd, David J. *King David: Innocent Blood and Bloodguilt*. Oxford: Oxford University Press, 2023.

Short, J. Randall. *The Surprising Election and Confirmation of King David*. Harvard Theological Studies 63. Cambridge: Harvard University Press, 2010.

Sternberg, Meir. *The Poetics of Biblical Narrative: Ideological Literature and the Drama of Reading*. Indiana Studies in Biblical Literature. Bloomington: Indiana University Press, 1985.

Steussy, Marti J. *David: Biblical Portraits of Power*. Studies on Personalities of the Old Testament. Columbia: University of South Carolina Press, 1999.

Stulac, Daniel J. D. *Gift of the Grotesque: A Christological Companion to the Book of Judges*. Eugene, OR: Cascade, 2022.

———. *Life, Land, and Elijah in the Book of Kings*. Cambridge: Cambridge University Press, 2021.

———. *Tragedy of the Commons: A Christological Companion to the Book of 1 Samuel*. Eugene, OR: Cascade, 2023.

———. "Wisdom That Delivers: Resurrection and Hope in the Book of Kings." *Horizons in Biblical Theology* 41 (2019) 25–50.

Stulac, Daniel J. D., and David A. Smith. "David, Uriah, Jesus, and Judas: An Intertestamental Pattern of Betrayal." *Journal of Theological Interpretation* 16 (2022) 223–33.

Thornton, Timothy C. G. "Solomonic Apologetic in Samuel and Kings." *Church Quarterly Review* 169.371 (1968) 159–66.

Tsumura, David Toshio. *The Second Book of Samuel*. The New International Commentary on the Old Testament. Grand Rapids: Eerdmans, 2019.

Van Seters, John. *The Biblical Saga of King David*. Winona Lake, IN: Eisenbrauns, 2009.

BIBLIOGRAPHY

———. "The Court History and DtrH: Conflicting Perspectives on the House of David." In *Die sogenannte Thronfolgegeschichte Davids: Neue Einsichten und Anfragen*, edited by Albert de Pury, 70–93. Orbis Biblicus et Orientalis 176. Göttingen: Vandenhoeck & Ruprecht, 2000.

Vowell, Sarah. *Take the Cannoli: Stories from the New World*. New York: Simon & Schuster, 2000.

Whitelam, Keith W. "The Defence of David." *Journal for the Study of the Old Testament* 9.29 (1984) 61–87.

Whitman, Walt. *Song of Myself (1892 Version)*. https://www.poetryfoundation.org/poems/45477/song-of-myself-1892-version.

Whybray, R. N. *The Succession Narrative: A Study of II Samuel 9–20; I Kings 1 and 2*. Studies in Biblical Theology II/9. London: SCM, 1968.

Wijk-Bos, Johanna W. H. van. *Reading Samuel: A Literary and Theological Commentary*. Macon, GA: Smyth & Helwys, 2011.

Wolpe, David. *David: The Divided Heart*. Jewish Lives. New Haven: Yale University Press, 2014.

www.ingramcontent.com/pod-product-compliance
Lightning Source LLC
Chambersburg PA
CBHW020933180426
43192CB00036B/949